2

Criticism and Truth

ROLAND BARTHES

Criticism and Truth

Translated and Edited by
KATRINE PILCHER KEUNEMAN

Foreword by
PHILIP THODY

THE ATHLONE PRESS
LONDON

First published in Great Britain, 1987
by the Athlone Press, 44 Bedford Row,
London WC1R 4LY

Originally published as *Critique et Vérité*,
by Editions du Seuil, Paris, 1966

British Library Cataloguing in Publication Data
Barthes, Roland,
Criticism and truth
1. Criticism 2. Linguistics
3. French literature – History and
criticism
I. Title II Critique et verite. *English*
801, '95 PN98.L/

ISBN 0–485–11321–X

Typesetting by TJB Photosetting Ltd, Lincolnshire
Printed in Great Britain at the University Press, Cambridge

Contents

Foreword

What do you do when you are shown, at least to the satisfaction of your opponents, to have written a book which puts forward a serious misreading of a major writer?

This, late in 1965, was the situation of the French critic Roland Barthes when Jean-François Revel chose to publish in his collection 'Libertés' an expanded version of an article which had first appeared earlier in the same year in the January-February number of *La Revue des Sciences Humaines*. The author of what had originally been entitled 'Nouvelle Critique ou Nouvelle Délire' was Raymond Picard, whose very scholarly account of Racine as a literary man in *La Carrière de Jean Racine* had been published in 1956 and led to his being appointed to the Chair of French Literature at the Sorbonne. Without Jean-François Revel's initiative, Picard's attack would probably have remained relatively unknown outside the academic world. It had not, perhaps rather unexpectedly, appeared in the highly traditional *Revue d'Histoire Littéraire de la France*, but in a more sociological journal which was edited at the time by an independently-minded Protestant called Albert-Marie Schmidt. The charges against Barthes were none the less put forward with some vigour, and expounded in the national press with some venom. What was Barthes to do?

The French love a good literary quarrel, especially if it

has ideological or political overtones. Throughout the twenties and thirties, the Surrealists had provided plenty of copy, and in the period immediately following the Second World War, Jean-Paul Sartre and his followers had made Existentialism probably the best-known word in the history of philosophical controversy. Sartre's own notoriety in this area reached its peak in 1952 with his public quarrel with Albert Camus about the latter's attack on Communism in *L'Homme révolté*, and connoisseurs with longer memories of arguments among men of letters would compare the performance of both authors with that of their forebears in earlier disputes in the seventeenth century between the Ancients and the Moderns. The argument in the eighteenth century between Voltaire and Rousseau, the struggles between supporters of Classicism and Romanticism in the early nineteenth century, and the insults exchanged in the controversies surrounding Naturalism, Symbolism and Impressionism were also still very much part of the folk memory of intellectual France, and the Barthes-Picard dispute seemed to promise another and possibly even livelier chapter in the entertaining spectacle whereby the French nailed their opponents as well as their theses to the church door of Saint-Germain-des-Prés.

Perhaps wisely, Barthes refused to oblige. Instead of taking up Picard's somewhat acerbic criticisms and responding with a comparably mordant wit, he moved the debate on to higher ground. The reply which he published in February 1966 under the title of *Critique et vérité*, and which is appearing for the first time in English in this translation by Katrine Pilcher Keuneman, concentrated on the question of the kind of language which can or should be used in literary criticism. For Raymond

Picard, as for the journalists who leaped forward to support him in the articles to which Barthes referred in one of his footnotes, this was not an issue which they were in the habit of discussing. The natural assumption, for them, was that the critic should use what they thought of as 'clear language'. This, in their view, had the advantage of having developed over the years, and therefore of having been used by some illustrious predecessors. It was also, in their view, immediately understandable to anyone with a reasonable education. It was neutral, in the sense of being sufficiently flexible to express a wide variety of ideas. And – most important of all – it was free from jargon.

Barthes's reply, couched in the kind of language which he had made peculiarly his own, was to say that no way of speaking could possibly have all these characteristics. The supposedly neutral language of Picard and of the journalists who had joined him in his criticism of the new French criticism was, he argued, just as full of presupposition as the style in which *Sur Racine* or any other work of the 'New Criticism' had been written. In his very first book, *Le Degré zéro de l'écriture* (*Writing Degree Zero*), first published in 1953, Barthes had insisted on the idea that the language commonly used in French intellectual discourse was essentially class-related, and corresponded to a particular set of social and philosophical attitudes. This is not a view peculiar to Barthes. In 1923, Marcel Proust wrote in *Le Côté de Guermantes* that it 'is difficult, when one's mind is troubled by the ideas of Kant and the nostalgia of Baudelaire, to write the exquisite French of Henri IV'. He then added a comment about one of his most elegant heroines, Oriane de Guermantes, which again anticipates one of the central points in Barthes's argument: 'the very purity of her language was a sign of limitation, so that, in her, both intelligence and sensibility had been closed against innovation'. The attempt to change the style in which artistic and intellectual issues are discussed in France has been going on for a long time, and *Critique et vérité* can be seen in this respect as part of a fairly long-running discussion.

As far as Barthes and his supporters were concerned, it was not only or even mainly a literary dispute. It had important educational, social and political implications as well. Looked at in the intellectual atmosphere of the 1980s, almost twenty years after the great shake-up of French social and intellectual life in the student rebellion of 1968, it is easy to see the dispute between Barthes and Picard as a prelude to those more dramatic and public events. On the one side, there is the French intellectual establishment, trying to maintain the traditions which had flourished in French academic life in the nineteenth and early twentieth centuries. On the other, there are the ideas which were to become much more widely acceptable in France after 1968. For although the events of May and June of that year were a political failure in that General de Gaulle remained in power and the constitution of the Fifth Republic survived intact, they did herald a series of fundamental social changes and the arrival of a much more open and eclectic intellectual atmosphere. *Nouvelle Critique ou nouvelle imposture* would be unlikely to receive as enthusiastic a welcome today as it did in 1965.

To the English-speaking reader, the interest of Barthes's reply in *Critique et vérité* is accompanied by a cultural as well as an intellectual and linguistic challenge. Barthes's own frame of reference is European, and primarily French. He refers to Noam Chomsky's *Syntactic Structures*, and he quotes Umberto Eco, Sigmund Freud and

Franz Kafka. But he does not refer to any English-speaking literary critics – Roman Jakobson, as Katrine Pilcher Keuneman's notes remind us, was born in Russia – and he does not quote the example of any poets, novelists or playwrights who have written in English. The writers he mentions are Proust, Mallarmé and Rimbaud, and his framework is that of the cultural and literary history of France.

It is a sign of the vigour and receptiveness of English-speaking culture that so many of Barthes's works should have appeared in translation, and that his ideas should have inspired so much critical activity in England, North America and Australasia. But it is not immediately obvious how his ideas can inform or renovate the tradition of the literary criticism which deals with Jane Austen, Dickens or Shakespeare. There is an obvious applicability to writers like James Joyce or Samuel Beckett, and contemporary novelists such as John Fowles and David Lodge clearly owe a considerable debt to the style of thinking about prose fiction which Barthes was one of the first to develop. But the tradition against which he is rebelling is not one which has been especially marked in the literary criticism published in England and America. In order to see what Barthes might mean in the English-speaking world, you need to look at how philosophers use language.

Thus it has been regarded as axiomatic, ever since the rise of logical positivism in the 1930s and the subsequent development of linguistic analysis, that philosophers should write as clearly as possible, with as many references as possible to the ordinary world. A. J. Ayer's *Language, Truth and Logic*, like Gilbert Ryle's *Dilemmas* or *The Problem of Mind*, carried out the progression which

Wittgenstein recommended when he wrote, in his *Tractatus Logico-Philosophicus*, in 1922, that 'everything that can be put into words can be put clearly' (4.116) and concluded the book with the phrase: 'what we cannot speak about one must consign to silence'. As Raymond Williams pointed out in a lecture about Lucien Goldmann, another of the French 'new critics', there has always been a tendency for British thinkers in the field of the humanities to be 'continually pulled back to ordinary language', and expected to make their views clear to any of their colleagues in medicine or the sciences who might drop in for a chat about Structuralism or Phenomenology on his way over to lunch. This has certainly tended to be the case in English universities, and Raymond Williams made a point which is highly applicable to the Barthes-Picard debate when he said that any 'break with the English bourgeoisie' would 'demand alternative procedures and styles'.

For although I myself have considerable sympathy with the style of philosophical writing which does in fact go further back than Wittgenstein, to David Hume and Bertrand Russell, I can see that such a preference is based upon the presupposition that the sceptically-minded, rationalistic, Anglo-Saxon professional middle classes are going to stay in power. Although Barthes was not a politically committed writer in the sense that Jean-Paul Sartre was, he did form part of that current in French thinking which sees the end of the dominance of society by the bourgeoisie as both inevitable and desirable. And since he maintained, throughout his career, that language is power, he wished to begin the disintegration and removal of this class by a critique of its language.

Critique et vérité thus has a wider interest than its

immediate applicability to the world of French studies, literary criticism and French classical literature. Katrine Pilcher Keuneman has translated it in a style which matches Barthes's own style of writing, and which consequently illustrates the kind of challenge which his thinking represents. In *Le Degré zéro de l'écriture* Barthes argued that the classical prose which both embodies and expresses the world view of the French middle class was first developed in the seventeenth century. Although it now seems, as Barthes would say, the most 'natural' way of expressing oneself, it may well have seemed as strange to people at the time as Barthes's own language still does to some people today.

Philip Thody

Preface to English-Language Edition

Towards the end of 1965 Raymond Picard, a professor at the Sorbonne, published a short monograph entitled *Nouvelle Critique ou nouvelle imposture*,[1] in which he attacks a whole group of so-called 'new critics', (Poulet, Richard, Goldmann, Mauron, etc., representatives of a movement in French criticism in the 1950s and 1960s called 'la nouvelle critique'). Picard, however, reserves the main blast of his criticism for Roland Barthes, at that time Director of Studies at the Ecole pratique des Hautes Etudes. Barthes had published in 1963 *Sur Racine*,[2] a collection of three essays partly in the psychoanalytic mode, though as Barthes points out in his introduction he is analysing the world created by Racine and not the author himself. In 1964 Barthes had published another collection of essays, *Essais critiques*.[3] In 'Les deux Critiques' he distinguished between interpretative (or new) criticism on the one hand and traditional or university criticism on the other. University criticism, says Barthes, seeks to

---

1 R. Picard, *Nouvelle Critique ou nouvelle imposture*, Pauvert, Utrecht, 1965; *New criticism or new fraud*? trs. F. Towne, Washington State University Press, 1969.
2 R. Barthes, *Sur Racine*, Seuil, 1963; *On Racine*, trs. Richard Howard, Hill & Wang, New York, 1964.
3 R. Barthes, *Essais critiques*, Seuil, 1964; *Critical Essays*, trs. Richard Howard, Northwestern University Press, 1972.

establish the facts surrounding the work but does not establish an interpretative framework for the work itself; it is based on an outdated positivist psychology of character; and it derives its explanation of the work from the (false) postulate of analogy – which always seeks to explain the work by reference to an 'elsewhere' of literature (another work, a historical circumstance, a passion experienced by the author).

Picard thus launches his own attack on the basis of a number of stances already adopted by Barthes. I shall not attempt to summarize all the points made by Picard against Barthes but principally those which Barthes takes up in *Criticism and Truth*. First, Picard accuses Barthes of violating the postulate of analogy mentioned above by practising (and defending, in others) a mode of criticism based on something external to the work. Then Picard says that, contrary to Barthes's view that in criticism the choice is between competing subjectivities, there *is* objective knowledge in literary criticism. Two extracts may be illuminating:

> Racine's words have a literal meaning which audiences and readers of the seventeenth century had to accept, and which cannot be ignored unless language is turned into a game of chance.

> There is a Racinian truth, upon which everyone can manage to agree. Basing himself especially on the certainties of language, on the implications of psychological coherence, on the requirements imposed by the structure of the genre, the modest and patient scholar manages to draw out a certain number of indisputable facts which as it were define areas of objectivity.[4]

Picard goes on to accuse Barthes of using obscure language and jargon; he also claims that Barthes's criticism in *On Racine* is impressionistic and dogmatic. Finally, Picard says that literature is not to be considered, as psychoanalysis would have it, the result of dark unconscious forces. Rather it ought to be considered as a reality in its own right, the result of a voluntary, clear intention to produce a work with a specific function and belonging to a certain genre. The meaning of the work lies in its controlled, structured patterns, which correspond, furthermore, to what the author has consciously chosen.

In *Criticism and Truth* Barthes makes some general points against Picard as well as debating points of detail. One of the more important general – and partly implicit – claims that Barthes makes is that criticism necessarily involves value judgments. Picard, Barthes is suggesting, wants to mask the ideological nature of his own position by invoking objectivity and truth in his own defence. (We can see a direct connection here with the notion that Barthes developed in *Mythologies*[5] that bourgeois ideology is an ideology which refuses to allow itself to be identified as an ideology by presenting itself as neutral, impartial, universal, objective and value-free.)

Barthes attacks, then, under a number of different headings, what I shall call the ideology of traditional French criticism. Let us look at them briefly.

---

4 Picard, *Nouvelle critique*, pp. 66, 69 – my translations.

5 R. Barthes, *Mythologies*, Seuil, 1957; *Mythologies*, partial English translation by Annette Lavers, Cape, 1972; Hill & Wang, 1973. Remaining essays, *The Eiffel Tower and Other Mythologies*, trs. Richard Howard, Hill & Wang, 1979.

Critical verisimilitude

Just as some works of literature are interpreted in accordance with verisimilitude, namely, what the reading public thinks likely or possible, so in criticism, says Barthes, there exists a kind of verisimilitude. What justifies criticism, according to this unspoken ideology, is common practice, common sense and that which goes without saying. The presuppositions of this critical method become apparent when it discovers supposed transgressions against its rules. It then reacts with exaggerated astonishment and claims that all deviations from itself are alarming, monstrous, pathological.

Objectivity

The meaning of words

Barthes denies that in his criticism he makes elementary mistakes regarding the meaning of words, as Picard accused him of doing.

Rather, Barthes feels entitled to take the dictionary meaning of words (say the now obsolete meaning of 'respirer' in seventeenth-century French) as a starting-point for a whole system of secondary or multiple meanings based on associations.

Psychological coherence

We must feel free, says Barthes, to interpret characters in classical literature in the light of the new kinds of psychological analysis developed in the twentieth century. The psychological coherence of a character is not *given*, it is a construct depending on the intellectual world and the value system of the judging mind. Any psychological perspective is always historically particular – including Picard's one of applying supposedly unchanging categories of analysis (looking at Racinian characters, for example, in terms of 'frenzy', 'passion', etc.).

The structure of the genre as an explanatory principle
Although Barthes allows that French classical tragedy may have a well-defined structure explained by its theorists, he claims that in most cases the genre in literature is not defined. Certainly it is not given once and for all. The very word *structure* itself opens up vistas of disagreement, for it is a methodological choice to perceive a structure in a work.

Good taste

'Old' criticism (as Barthes somewhat mockingly calls traditional criticism) is itself based on a system of taboos, according to Barthes. However, it also operates a particular set of taboos governing the sorts of things one may write about. Thus the critic J.-P. Richard is ridiculed by old criticism for talking of spinach in connection with Stendhal – he has violated the taboo against the concrete in literary discourse. 'Good taste' allows the old critic to reject any discourse he does not like – once again, in terms of an undefended aesthetic.

All talk of sexuality is particularly subject to taboo, and this is partly because old criticism has an outmoded, simplistic concept of the human mind and body, sharply divided into upper and lower, controlled and inchoate, conscious and anarchistic.

Clarity

The value placed on clarity is also ideologically based. Old criticism's liking for clarity is a kind of political approval by a class of its own language.

The so-called jargon of new criticism cannot in fact be defined by its inherent qualities – for old criticism too indulges in floweriness. Rather it is the case that the language of the other, but not its own language, is perceived as jargon by old criticism.

In the last analysis Barthes denies that clarity is something separate that can be imposed on a discourse from the outside.

The inability to think symbolically

Barthes sees old criticism as suffering from a specific disorder – the incapacity to think symbolically. The old critics, says Barthes, are caught in the literal reading they give to texts. Since they cannot go beyond the letter to the symbol, they cannot, in effect, read, since reading is properly symbolic.

Whether we interpret language 'literally' or 'symbolically' (and ultimately Barthes appears to be suggesting that there is no hard and fast line between the two) constitutes a methodological choice. A symbolic reading is not a deviation from 'evident truth'. There *is* rigour in literary criticism, insists Barthes, but the rigour consists not in the choice of code but in a consistent reading once one has chosen a code.

In the second part of *Criticism and Truth*, Barthes is at first still implicitly arguing in opposition to Picard's simplistic notion of criticism. Whereas Picard views literature as having an objectively verifiable meaning derived from an examination of the meaning of words in the historical period when they were written, for Barthes, on the contrary, criticism has been going through a crisis for the hundred years since Mallarmé.

This crisis, which Barthes calls the 'crisis of commentary', flows from the fact that writers such as Proust and Blanchot have brought us to see that the boundaries between creative writing on the one hand and criticism on the other do not really exist. A writer cannot be defined by his status, the official role which society gives him, but only by a certain awareness of discourse. The writer is the person for whom language is problematical, not transparent, who lays emphasis on the depths and not the instrumentality of language.

Language does not have a single meaning given by the dictionary and the historical age which gave rise to the work. An age may believe that it alone holds the canonical meaning of a work, but meanings are different across history and among different readers. The meaning of language is not singular but plural. This is so because of the very structure of language and not through some infirmity in those who read.

In explaining the ramifications of his own theory of reading and criticism Barthes then largely leaves behind the specific quarrel with Picard. He formulates a three-sided view of the nature of our relationship with a work. We can adopt three discourses 'to weave a garland of language'[6] around the work: *science*, *criticism*, *reading*.

The *science of literature*, says Barthes, is a general dis-

6 Below, p. 73

course whose object is not a particular meaning of the work but the very plurality of its meanings. This science will base itself on the ramifications of the fact that a work is constructed out of written language. Just as Chomsky developed the idea of a generative grammar of language giving the principles governing construction of sentences in a language, so Barthes foreshadows the development of a science defining the conditions of existence of the contents of a work, of a generative grammar of the possible meanings of a work.

The science of literature will throw into doubt the very notion of an author as source and guarantor of the meaning of the work.[7] Literary science will liberate the work from the constraints of the author's intention in order to relate it to its real origins, which are mythological. The author may be the origin of the work but the work is in reality inhabited by a vast mythical and human significance which should not be located in the author.

Criticism on the other hand is not a science. Science is concerned with meanings in general, criticism produces particular meanings. Criticism is a discourse which engenders a meaning and attaches it to a form, the work. It cannot 'translate' the work but merely attaches a coherent set of signs to it.

Although criticism imprints an anamorphosis (distorted image) on the work, *all* such projections are in fact distorted, for the work is not an object which can reflect its own meaning. What limits the critic then is not 'the

---

7 Barthes develops this notion further in a later article, 'La Mort de l'auteur', *Manteia*, V, 1968, pp. 12–17: 'The Death of the Author', trs. Stephen Heath in *Image-Music-Text* S. Heath (ed.), Fontana, 1977.

meaning' of the work (which in fact cannot 'correct' a critic's viewpoint) but only the meaning of his or her own statements.

However, contrary to Picard's claim that if Picard's particular pretensions to objectivity are abandoned then the critic can say 'anything at all' about a work, Barthes considers that criticism does still operate within a set of constraints.

The specific limiting constraints are: first, everything in a work is intelligible, and critical discourse must be able to account for all of it. This 'rule of exhaustiveness' ought not to be confused with Picard's system of statistical verification – which is supposed to establish what we are entitled to assert but is less scientific than it appears to be. How often must an idea or a theme recur in an author's works before we are justified in making a generalization about it? Barthes believes that this question is answered not by science or statistics, as Picard claims, but by an act of choice on the part of the critic, who must himself decide that a meaningful pattern has emerged.

Secondly, criticism operates transformations according to laws, claims Barthes. There is a logic of the signifier even though it may not be well known and even though we are not clear what kind of 'knowledge' it may be the object of. However, some transformational models are given us by psychoanalysis and rhetoric. Critics thus seek in the work regulated and not random transformations across a linked group of units; they are looking for the work's symbolic logic.

Thirdly, criticism must move always in the same direction ('aller dans le même sens'.)[8] The dispute is not actually one (as Picard would have it) between subjectivity and objectivity in criticism, for a cultivated subjectivity, acting under constraints themselves emanating from the work, may come closer to the literary object than an uncultivated and literal-minded 'objectivity'.

Although Barthes does not spell out the connection in so many words, this third constraint appears to link up with the requirement that a critic's work be internally consistent, which Barthes articulates in Part I.

Reading is the third discourse which surrounds the work. Reading is to be distinguished from criticism. The critic at the very least re-articulates a thought (and thus plays a role in its transmission); critics also redistribute the elements of a book by their fracturing and re-presentation of it. Critics must also commit themselves by virtue of having chosen to commit words to paper.

Reading, however, seems to involve a more subtle relationship to the text in Barthes's view; it is a relationship based on desire, which lies outside the code of language.

Although *Criticism and Truth* starts out as a defence of French 'new criticism', some of whose practitioners (like J.–P. Richard and Charles Mauron) plainly believe that there is an important authorial presence behind works of literature which serves in part at least to explain those works, as Barthes progresses through the book the centre of interest shifts to the problem of the relationship between subject and language. Thus the author as such disappears and becomes a void around which an infinitely transformed discourse is woven.

Indeed, Barthes cannot show us how to extricate ourselves from this web of language, claiming as he does that

8 Below, p. 84

in the last analysis the critic confronts an object which is not the work but his or her own language.[9]

Barthes is an immensely well-read man who assumes a wide general knowledge in his reader. Writing for a cultivated French audience, he presumes that it shares his familiarity with the French classics and the French critical tradition; he also presupposes that the historical memories of his readers and their cultural framework resemble his own. Because of this, the average English-speaking reader is likely to feel somewhat remote from Barthes's intellectual world and may welcome some help in following up the many philosophical, literary and critical references, whether to obscure or better-known figures.

I have therefore provided a set of notes on some of the ideas, events and people referred to in Barthes's text. Words or names on which a note is given are marked with an asterisk the first time they appear in the text, and the notes are listed in alphabetical order at the end of the book.

Although, on one level, Barthes's argument in *Criticism and Truth* is logically self-contained, it is also clear that his exposition acquires greater depth and meaning when placed in its cultural context. It is hoped that the background notes go some way towards providing that context.

Katrine Pilcher Keuneman

9 Below, p. 85

I

What is called 'new criticism' has existed for some time. Since the Liberation (as was to be expected), a certain reappraisal of our classical literature has been undertaken under the influence of new philosophies, by critics of widely differing persuasions and across a great range of monographs which in the end have covered the whole gamut of our authors from Montaigne to Proust. We should not be surprised that a country should periodically review in this way the things which come down from its past and describe them anew in order to find out *what it can make of them*: such activities are and ought to be normal assessment procedures.

Now, however, people have suddenly accused this movement of fraud,[1] casting upon its works (or at least certain of them) those taboos which normally define, by rejecting them, what all avant-garde movements are: people have discovered that these works are intellectually empty, verbally sophisticated, morally dangerous and that they owe their success to snobbery alone. The surprising thing is that these accusations should come so

1 R. Picard, *Nouvelle critique ou nouvelle imposture* (Paris, J.J. Pauvert, Collection 'Libertés', 1965), p. 149. Raymond Picard's attacks are directed mainly against R. Barthes, *Sur Racine* (Seuil, 1963).

late. Why today? Is it an unimportant reaction? The return to the offensive of a certain obscurantism? Or on the contrary the first resistance to new forms of discourse which are being evolved and whose existence has been suspected?

What is striking about the recent attacks on new criticism is their immediately and apparently instinctively collective character.[2] Something primitive and bare has begun to stir in all this. One might have thought one was witnessing a primitive rite of exclusion of a dangerous individual from an archaic community. Hence the strange vocabulary of *execution*.[3] People have dreamed of *wounding* new criticism, *pricking* its pretensions, *assaulting* it, *murdering* it, dragging it before the *criminal courts*, setting it in the *pillory* or putting it on the *scaffold*.[4] A very sensitive point had no doubt been raised since the executioner was not merely praised for his talent, but *thanked*, congratulated like a dispenser of justice at the end of a cleanup: he had already been promised immor-

---

2 A certain group of journalists has given Picard's libel uncritical, total and unreserved support. Let us print the roll of honour of old criticism (since there is new criticism): *Les Beaux Arts* (Brussels, 23 Dec. 1965), *Carrefour* (29 Dec. 1965), *La Croix* (10 Dec. 1965), *Le Figaro* (3 Nov. 1965), *Le XXe siècle* (Nov. 1965), *Midi libre* (18 Nov. 1965), *Le Monde* (23 Oct. 1965), to which we must add certain of its readers' letters (13, 20, 27 Nov. 1965), *La Nation française* (28 Oct. 1965), *Pariscope* (27 Oct. 1965), *La Revue Parlementaire* (15 Nov. 1965), *Europe-Action* (Jan. 1966); not forgetting the Académie Française (Marcel Achard's reply to Thierry Maulnier, *Le Monde*, 21 Jan. 1966).

3 'It's an execution' (*La Croix*).

tality, now they are embracing him.[5] In short the 'execution' of new criticism has the appearance of a job belonging to public health, which was bravely undertaken and whose successful completion affords relief.

Coming from a limited group, these attacks bear a kind of ideological stamp, they plunge into that ambiguous area of culture where something unfailingly political, though separate from the political choices of the day, infiltrates judgment and language.[6] During the Second Empire* new criticism would have been put on trial: does

---

4 Here are some of these gratuitously offensive images: 'the arms of ridicule' (*Le Monde*); 'correction by a sound birching' (*Nation française*); 'well-directed blow', 'deflating unsightly gourds' (*Le XXe siècle*); 'the charge of murderous spearheads' (*Le Monde*); 'intellectual fraud' (R. Picard, *op. cit.*); 'Pearl Harbour of new criticism' (*Revue de Paris*, Jan. 1966); 'Barthes in the pillory' (*L'Orient*, Beirut, 16 Jan. 1966); 'wring new criticism's neck and decapitate properly a certain number of impostors including Mr Roland Barthes, whose cleanly cut-off head you are brandishing' (*Pariscope*).

5 'I think for my part that the works of Mr Barthes will date more quickly than those of Mr Picard' (E. Guitton, *Le Monde*, 28 March 1964). 'I should like to embrace Mr Raymond Picard for having written...your pamphlet (*sic*)' (Jean Cau, *Pariscope*).

6 'Raymond Picard replies here to the progressive Roland Barthes...Picard silences those who replace classic analysis by the superimposition of their verbal delirium, those maniacs of interpretation who think that everyone reasons as they do with reference to the Càbbala, the Pentateuch or Nostradamus. The excellent series "Libertés", produced by Jean-François Revel (with books on Diderot, Celse, Rougier, Russell), will cause yet more gnashing of teeth, though not of ours' (*Europe-Action*, Jan. 1966).

it not affront reason by disobeying the '*elementary rules of scientific or even simply articulated thought*'? Does it not shock morality in the way it brings into everything '*an obsessive, unbridled, cynical sexuality*'? Does it not discredit our national institutions in the eyes of foreigners?[7] In a word, is it not '*dangerous*'?[8] When a word like dangerous is applied to ideas, language or art, it immediately signals a desire to return to the past. It means that the speaker is fearful (hence the unity we find in the images of destruction); the speaker fears all innovation, which he denounces on each occasion as 'empty' (in general that is all that can be found to be said about what is new). However this traditional fear is complicated today by the contrary fear of appearing anachronistic; suspicion towards the new is combined with a few nods in the direction of '*the call of the present*' or the necessity to '*rethink the problems of criticism*'; '*the vain return to the past*'[9] is dismissed with a fine oratorical gesture. Regressiveness appears shameful today, just like capitalism.[10] Whence come remarkable *jerks and abrupt halts*: there is a pretence for a while of accepting modern works, which

---

7 Picard, pp.58, 30, 84.

8 Picard, pp.85, 148.

9 E. Guitton, *Le Monde*, 13 Nov. 1965; Picard, p.149; J. Piatier, *Le Monde*, 23 Oct. 1965.

10 Five hundred supporters of J.L. Tixier-Vignancour state in a manifesto their determination to 'pursue their action on the base of a militant organization and a nationalist ideology... capable of effectively opposing Marxism and capitalist technocracy' (*Le Monde*, 30–31 Jan. 1966).

one ought to discuss since they are being discussed; then, suddenly, a sort of limit having been reached, people proceed to a joint execution. These trials, set up periodically by closed groups, are thus in no way extraordinary; they happen at the end of certain disturbances of equilibrium. But why, today, Criticism?

What is worthy of note in this operation is not so much that it sets up the old against the new, it is rather that, in an unmasked reaction, it casts a taboo upon a certain kind of discourse about a book: what is not tolerated is that language should talk about language.

Discourse reflecting upon discourse is the object of a special vigilance on the part of institutions, which normally contain it within the limits of a strict code: in the literary State, criticism must be controlled as much as a police force is: to free the one would be quite as 'dangerous' as democratizing the other: it would be to threaten the power of power, the language of language. To do a second writing of the first writing of the work is indeed to open the way to unforeseeable relaying of meaning, the endless play of mirrors, and it is this room for manoeuvre which is suspect.

So long as criticism had the traditional function of judging, it could not but be conformist, that is to say in conformity with the interests of the judges. However, the true 'criticism' of institutions and languages does not consist in 'judging' them, but in *perceiving*, in *separating*, in *dividing*. To be subversive, the critic does not have to judge, it is enough that he talks of language instead of using it. What new criticism is reproached with today is not so much that it is 'new', but that it is fully 'criticism', that it re-allocates the roles of author and commentator and in so doing attacks the linguistic order.[11] One can be satisfied that this is the case if one looks at the law which is cited against it and which is invoked to justify its 'execution'.

Critical verisimilitude

Aristotle established the technique of mimetic discourse based on the existence of a certain *verisimilitude* deposited in the mind of men by tradition, Wise Men, the majority, current opinion, etc. What is convincing in a work or discourse is that which contradicts none of these authorities. Verisimilitude does not necessarily correspond to what was once the case (that is a matter for history) nor to what must be (that is a matter for science) but simply to what the public thinks is possible, which can be quite different from historical reality or scientific possibility. Aristotle based a certain aesthetics of readership on it; if one applied it today to works aimed at a mass audience one might perhaps be able to reconstruct what is the verisimilitude of our time; for such works never contradict what the audience thinks is possible, however historically or scientifically impossible that might be.

Old criticism is not unrelated to what one might think of as criticism for the masses, if ever our society started to consume critical commentaries in the way that it consumes films, novels or songs; as far as the general cultural community is concerned, it has a readership, reigns supreme in the literary pages of some big newspapers and moves in accordance with an intellectual logic which ordains that one may not contradict that which comes

11 Cf. *infra*, p. 63ff.

from tradition, from Wise Men, from current opinion, etc. In short, there is a kind of critical verisimilitude.

This verisimilitude is hardly ever expressed in declarations of principle. As it is that which *goes without saying* it never raises questions of method, since a method is, in a quite contrary way, the act of doubt by which one asks oneself about chance or nature. You notice it particularly when it adopts astonishment and indignation before the 'extravagances' of new criticism: everything appears to it as '*absurd*', '*bizarre*', '*aberrant*', '*pathological*', '*frenzied*', '*alarming*'.[12] Criticism based on verisimilitude is very fond of 'evident truths'. These evident truths are, however, essentially normative. By a habitual process of confused logic, the unbelievable proceeds from the forbidden, that is to say from the dangerous: disagreements become divergences, divergences become errors, errors

---

12 Here are the expressions applied by Picard to new criticism: 'fraud', 'the daring and the preposterous' (p.11), 'pedantically' (p.39), 'aberrant extrapolation' (p.40), 'intemperate manner, statements which are inaccurate, debatable or ridiculous' (p.47), 'pathological character of this language' (p.50), 'absurdities' (p.52), 'intellectual trickery' (p.54), book fit to arouse revulsion' (p.57), 'a surfeit of self-satisfied inconsistency', 'repertory of fallacies' (p.59), 'wild statements' (p.71), 'frightening lines' (p.73), 'extravagant doctrine' (p.73), 'laughable and empty intelligibility' (p.75), 'arbitary, inconsistent, absurd results' (p.92), 'absurdities and bizarreries' (p.146), 'gullibility' (p.147). I was going to add 'laboriously inaccurate', 'blunders', 'self-satisfaction which makes one smile', 'chinoiseries of form', 'subtleties of a deliquescent mandarin', etc., but those words are not Picard's, they are in Sainte-Beuve imitated by Proust and in the speech of Monsieur de Norpois 'disposing of' Bergotte...

become sins,[13] sins become illnesses, illnesses become monstrosities. As this normative system is very narrow, a mere nothing can go outside it: rules appear, perceptible at those limits of verisimilitude which one cannot transgress without coming up against a sort of critical *anti-nature* and falling into what is then called 'teratology'.[14] What then are the rules of critical verisimilitude in 1965?

Objectivity

The first such rule, which we are told about endlessly, is *objectivity*. What then is objectivity in literary criticism? What is the characteristic of a work which 'exists outside us'?[15] This *external thing* which is so precious since it must control the extravagance of the critic and about which we ought to be able to agree easily since it is removed from the variations of our thought, is given endless different definitions; once upon a time it was reason, nature, taste, etc.; more recently it has been the author's life, the 'laws of the genre', history. And now today we are given a different definition. We are told that the work of literature contains 'evident truths' which it is possible to draw forth by relying on '*the certainties of language, the implications of psychological coherence and the imperatives of the structure of the genre*'.[16]

---

13 A reader of *Le Monde*, in bizarrely religious terms, says that a certain book of new criticism 'is laden with sins against objectivity' (27 Nov. 1965).
14 Picard, p.88.
15 'Objectivity: term of modern philosophy. Quality of that which is objective; existence of objects outside ourselves' (Littré dictionary).
16 Picard, p.69.

The ghosts of several different models have merged here. The first is lexicographical: we must read Corneille, Racine, Molière, with Cayrou's *Le Français Classique*[§] at our sides. Yes, doubtless; who ever denied it? But once you know the meaning of words, what are you going to do with it? What are called (one would like it to have been said ironically) 'the certainties of language' are only the certainties of the French language, the certainties of the dictionary. The problem (or the pleasure) is that idiom is nothing but the material from which another language is constructed, *which does not contradict the first*, and which is full of uncertainties; to what instrument of verification, to what dictionary are you going to submit this profound, vast and symbolic second language, from which the work is made, and which is precisely the language of multiple meanings?[17] Similarly for 'psychological coherence'. With what key are you going to read it? There are several ways of naming human behaviour, and having named it, several ways of describing its coherence: the implications of psychoanalytical psychology are different from those of behaviourist psychology, etc. What remains as a last resort is 'current' psychology, which

§ Translator's note: Gaston Cayrou, *Le Français Classique. Lexique de la langue du 17e Siècle*, Paris, 1923.

17 Although I am not specially concerned to defend *On Racine* in particular, I cannot see repeated Jacqueline Piatier's claim in *Le Monde* (23 Oct. 1965) that I have misunderstood Racine's language. If, for example, I drew attention to the connection between *breathing* [*respiration*] and the verb *to breathe* [*respirer*] (Picard, p.53), it is not that I did not know the contemporary meaning (*to relax* [*se détendre*]), as I said in any event (*Sur Racine*, p.57), it is that the lexicographical meaning

everyone can recognize, thus acquiring a strong feeling of security. Misfortune would have it that that particular psychology is made up of all we were taught at school about Racine, Corneille, etc. – which amounts to interpreting an author in the light of the acquired image we have of him: a fine tautology! To say that the characters (of *Andromaque*) are '*frenzied people the violence of whose passion*, etc.'[18] is to substitute platitude for absurdity without however guaranteeing that error has been avoided. As for the 'structure of the genre', one would like to know more about it: for a hundred years people have discussed the word 'structure'; there are several structuralisms: genetic, phenomenological, etc.; there is also a 'student's' structuralism, which consists in giving the 'plan' of a work. Which structuralism are we talking about? How can we find the structure without the help of a methodological model? Perhaps we can manage to find the structure of French tragedy, whose canons are known

---

did not contradict the symbolic meaning, which is in the event and quite perversely, the *first* meaning. On this point, as on many others, where Picard's pamphlet, followed unchecked by his allies, interprets things in the most unfavourable way possible, I shall pray Proust to reply, recalling what he wrote to Paul Souday, who had accused him of using incorrect French: 'My book may reveal an absence of talent; but at least it presupposes, it implies enough general education for there to be no intellectual likelihood of my making such gross errors as those which you have pointed out' (*Choix de Lettres*, Plon, 1965, p.196).

18 Picard, p.30.

thanks to the classical theorists; but what then will be the 'structure' of the novel, which we will have to contrast with the 'extravagances' of new criticism?

These 'evident truths' are thus only choices. Taken literally, the first is trivial or, of one prefers, could not ever be relevant; nobody has ever denied or will ever deny that the language of the text has a literal meaning, of which philology will, if necessary, inform us; what we need to know is whether or not one has the right to read in this literal language other meanings which do not contradict it; it is not the dictionary which will answer this question, but an overall decision on the symbolic nature of language. And similarly for the other 'evident truths': they are *already* interpretations, for they imply a pre-existing choice of psychological or structural model; this code – for it is a code – can vary; all the objectivity of the critic will depend then, not on the choice of code, but on the rigour with which he applies the model he has chosen to the work in question.[19] This is not a minor consideration; but since new criticism has never claimed anything else, basing the objectivity of its descriptions on their coherence, it was hardly worth the trouble of starting a war against new criticism. Critical verisimilitude usually chooses the code of literalness, which is a choice like any other. Let us see, however, what the consequences of that are.

It is said that we must '*preserve the meaning of words*',[20] in short that the word has only one meaning: the right one. This rule illicitly engenders a suspicion, or,

---

19 On this new objectivity, cf. *infra*, p. 78

20 Picard, p.45.

what is worse, a general trivialization of metaphorical language: sometimes it is purely and simply forbidden (we must not say that Titus murders Bérénice since Bérénice is not really murdered);[21] sometimes it is rendered ridiculous by a more or less ironic attempt to take it literally (that which links the sun-like Néron to the tears of Junie is reduced to the action of the '*sun which dries up a pond*'[22] or to a '*borrowing from astrology*');[23] sometimes one is not allowed to see in it anything other than cliché of a certain historical period (you are not allowed to feel the existence of breathing [*respiration*] in the verb to *breathe* [*respirer*] since the verb *respirer* in the seventeenth century meant *to relax*). One is thus brought to some strange lessons in reading: one must read poetry without *evoking* anything: it is forbidden to allow any perspective to rise from words as simple and concrete as port, harem, tears – however worn-out they may have already become in their own time. In the last analysis, words no longer have any referential value, only an exchange value: their function is to communicate, as in the dullest of transactions, not to suggest. In a word, language offers only one certainty: that of banality: therefore one always chooses banality.

Another victim of literalness: the character, object of a credence at once excessive and trivial; a character never has the right to be mistaken about itself or its feelings: dishonest excuse is a category unknown to critical verisimilitude (Oreste and Titus cannot lie to themselves), just as fantasy is unknown. (Eriphile doubtless loves Achille without ever imagining that she is possessed by

21 Ibid.

22 Picard, p.17.

23 *Revue parlementaire*, 15 Nov. 1965.

him.[24] This surprising clarity of beings and relationships is not confined to fiction; for critical verisimilitude, life itself is clear: the same banality governs the relationship of people in books and in the world. It is said that there is no interest in seeing in Racine's work a theatre of Captivity, since that is a common situation;[25] similarly, it is pointless to insist on the power game which Racinian tragedy portrays on stage, since, we are reminded, all societies are based on power.[26] That is really to view with a great deal of equanimity the presence of power in human relationships. Literature itself is less blasé; it has never failed to comment on the *intolerable* character of banal situations, since literature is precisely the discourse which makes of an ordinary relationship a fundamental relationship and transforms that into an outrageous relationship. Thus critical verisimilitude devotes itself to dropping everything down a notch: what is banal in life must not be heightened; what is not banal in the work must on the other hand be banalized: singular aesthetic this, which condemns life to silence and the work to insignificance.

Good taste

Moving on to the other rules of critical verisimilitude, we must descend even lower, come up against derisory censure, enter into out-of-date quarrels, dialogue, through

24 Picard, p.33.
25 Picard, p.22.
26 Picard, p.39.

today's old critics, with the old critics of the day before yesterday, Nisard* or Népomucène Lemercier.*

What shall we call this group of interdictions which belong to both ethics and aesthetics and in which classical criticism invests all those values which it cannot claim to be knowledge? Let us call this system of prohibitions *good taste*.[27] What does good taste forbid us to speak of? Of objects. When it is transported into rational discourse, the object is supposed to be vulgar: it is an incongruity whose source is not the objects themselves but the mixture of abstract and concrete (it is always forbidden to mix things that are different); what appears ridiculous is that one can talk of *spinach* in connection with *literature*;[28] it is the distance between the object and the codified language of criticism which is shocking. Thus one ends up with a strange exchanging of positions: while old criticism's few pages are completely abstract[29] and the works of new criticism are on the contrary hardly abstract at all, since new criticism deals with substances and objects, it is new criticism which is, it seems, of an inhuman abstraction. In fact, what verisimilitude calls 'concrete' is only, yet again, what is customary. What is customary defines good taste as perceived by verisimilitude; to satisfy versimilitude criticism should be composed neither of objects (they are too prosaic),[30] nor of ideas (they are too abstract), but only of values.

It is here that *good taste* is very useful: as a servant

27 Picard, p.32.

28 Picard, pp.110,135.

29 See Picard's prefaces to the tragedies of Racine, *Oeuvres complètes*, Pléiade, I, 1956.

30 In fact, too symbolic.

shared by ethics and aesthetics, it allows us to have a convenient turnstile connecting the Beautiful and the Good, discreetly merged in the form of a simple measure. However this measure has all the disappearing power of a mirage: when someone reproaches a critic for speaking excessively of sexuality, it should be understood that talking of sexuality is always excessive: to imagine for a moment that classical heroes might be equipped with (or not equipped with) sexual organs is to '*bring in at every turn*' an '*obsessive, unbridled, cynical*'[31] sexuality. The possibility that sexuality might have a precise (and not disruptive) role in the configuration of characters is not considered; that, furthermore, such a role might vary according to whether one follows Freud or Adler, for example, does not for one minute cross the mind of the old critic: what does he know about Freud other than what he has read in some slim paperback?

Good taste is in fact a taboo against using certain kinds of language. If psychoanalysis is condemned, it is not because it thinks but because it speaks; if one could confine it to being a purely medical practice and immobilize the patient (not the old critics themselves) on his couch, they would worry about it as little as they do about acupuncture. But now psychoanalysis turns its attention to the sacred being by definition (which they would like to be themselves), the writer. At a pinch one could dare to write psychoanalytically about a modern writer, but not about a classical one! Racine, the most limpid of poets, the most chaste of passionate writers![32]

---

31 Picard, p.30.

32 'Can one build on Racine, who is so clear, a new obscure way of judging and dismantling genius?' (*Revue parlementaire*, 15 Nov. 1965).

In fact, the image that old criticism has constructed of psychoanalysis is incredibly out-of-date. This image rests upon an archaic classification of the human body. Old criticism's man is thus made up of two anatomical zones. The first is, so to speak, superior-external: the head, artistic creation, noble appearance, that which can be shown, that which one ought to see; the second is inferior-internal: sex (which must not be named), instincts, '*impulses of the moment*', '*the organic*', '*anonymous automatisms*', '*the obscure world of anarchistic tensions*';[33] on the one hand the primitive, instinctual man, on the other the evolved and controlled author. Now, it is said indignantly, psychoanalysis wrongfully makes a connection between the top and the bottom, the inside and the outside; even more seriously it gives, so it seems, an exclusive privilege to the hidden 'lower part', which is becoming in new criticism, so we are assured, the explanatory principle of the visible 'upper part'. Thus we are taking the risk of no longer being able to separate '*pebbles*' from '*diamonds*'.[34] How can we correct such a puerile image? One would like to explain yet again to old criticism that psychoanalysis does not reduce its object to the 'unconscious';[35] that in consequence psychoanalytic

---

33 Picard, pp.135–6.

34 Since we are talking about precious stones, let us quote this gem: 'By always wanting to unearth a writer's obsession at any price, one takes the risk of going to dig for it in the "depths" where one can find all sorts of things, where one runs the risk of mistaking a pebble for a diamond' (*Midi libre*, 18 Nov. 1965).

criticism (contestable for quite different reasons, some of which are psychoanalytic) at least cannot be accused of creating for itself a '*dangerously passivist conception*'[36] of literature since, on the contrary, it considers the author to be the subject of *work* (a word which belongs to psychoanalytic language, let us not forget); that it is, in addition, a *petitio principii* to attribute greater worth to 'conscious thought' and to postulate as self-evident the low value of the '*immediate and elementary*'; and that besides, all these aesthetic-cum-moral distinctions between a man who is organic, impulsive, automatic, unformed, unrefined, obscure, etc., and a literature which is self-controlled, lucid, noble, glorious by virtue of its restraint of language, are quite simply stupid, given that psychoanalytic man is not geometrically divisible and that, following Jacques Lacan,* we may say that his topology is not that of the *inside* and the *outside*,[37] even less that of the *top* and the *bottom*, but rather that of a moving *obverse* and *reverse* whose language as a matter of fact never stops playing different roles and turning surfaces around something which, from beginning to end, does not actually exist. But what is the point of saying all this? The ignorance of old criticism with regard to psychoanalysis has all the solidity and tenacity of a myth (which is why it ends by being somewhat fascinating): it is not a refusal, it is an attitude of mind destined to travel imperturbably across the ages: '*Shall I tell of the assiduity of a whole school of literature which for fifty years, notably in France, has declaimed the primacy of instinct, the*

35 Picard, pp.122–3.
36 Picard, p.142.
37 Picard, p.128.

unconscious, intuition, will in the German sense, that is to say in contrast with intelligence.' That was not written in 1965 by Raymond Picard, but in 1927 by Julien Benda.[38]*

Clarity

Now we come to the last act of censure carried out by critical verisimilitude. As one might expect, it bears on language itself. Some forms of language are forbidden to the critic as being '*jargon*'. Only one form of language is allowed: '*clarity*'.[39]

For a long time now our French society has experienced clarity not as a simple quality of verbal communication, as a shifting attribute which can be applied to different modes of speech, but as a separate kind of locution: it is a matter of writing in a certain kind of sacred idiom, related to the French language, just as hieroglyphics, Sanskrit or medieval Latin were written.[40] The idiom in question, named 'French clarity' is a language

---

38 Quoted approvingly by *Midi Libre* (18 Nov. 1965). A small study could be done on the contemporary descendants of Julien Benda.

39 I forbear from quoting all the accusations of 'opaque jargon' which have been made against me.

40 This has all been said in an appropriate way by Raymond Queneau*: 'This algebra of Newtonian [humorously gallicized as '*nioutonien*'] rationalism, this Esperanto which facilitated the shady dealings of Catherine the Great and Frederick of Prussia, this argot of diplomats, Jesuits and Euclidean geometricians remains supposedly the prototype, the ideal and the measure of all varieties of French' (*Bâtons, chiffres et lettres*, Gallimard, 'Idées', 1965, p.50).

whose origin is political. It was born at a time when the upper classes hoped – in accordance with a well-known ideological practice – to convert the particularity of their writing into a universal idiom, persuading people that the 'logic' of French was an absolute logic: it was called the genius of the language: that of French consists in first presenting the subject, then the action and last of all the object, in conformity, so they said, with the 'natural' model. This myth has been scientifically dismantled by modern linguistics:[41] French is neither more nor less 'logical' than the next language.[42]

The many mutilations inflicted on our language by classical institutions are well-known. The strange thing is that the French never tire of priding themselves on their Racine (the man with the vocabulary of two thousand words) and never complain of not having had a Shakespeare of their own. Still today they fight with ridiculous passion for their 'French language': oracular chronicles, fulminations against foreign invasions, death sentences on certain supposedly unwanted words. We must endlessly clean, scrape off, forbid, eliminate, preserve. You could parody the medical terminology which traditional criticism uses to describe language it does not like (calling it 'pathological'), and say that we have here a kind of national illness, which we shall call *ablutionism of language*. We shall leave ethno-psychiatry the task of defining the

---

41 See Charles Bally, *Linguistique générale et Linguistique française*, Bern, Francke, 4th ed, 1965.

42 One should not confuse classicism's claim that French syntax is the best expression of universal logic with the profound views of the thinkers of Port Royal on the problems of language in general (taken up again today by N. Chomsky).

exact meaning of this phenomenon, though think it worth pointing out the rather sinister aspect of this verbal Malthusianism. '*In Papua*', says the geographer Baron, '*language is very impoverished: each tribe has its language and its vocabulary grows ever smaller because after each death several words are eliminated as a sign of mourning*'.[43] On this point we outdo the Papauns: we respectfully embalm the language of dead writers and reject the words and new meanings which appear in the world of ideas: in France, the signs of mourning accompany birth and not death.

Language taboos are part of a small war among intellectual castes. Old criticism is one caste among others, and the 'French clarity' it recommends is a jargon just like any other. It is a particular kind of language, written by a defined group of writers, critics and chroniclers; essentially it is a pastiche not even of our classical authors but only of the classicism of our writers. This backward-looking jargon is in no way shaped by precise requirements of reasoning or an ascetic absence of images, as can be the formal language of logic (it is only here that one would have the right to talk of 'clarity'), but by a community of stereotypes, sometimes twisted and overloaded to the point of bombast[44] by the predilection for certain exaggerated turns of phrase, and of course by a refusal of certain words, rejected with horror or irony as intruders

43 E. Baron, *Géographie*, Classe de Philosophie, Editions de l'Ecole, p.83.

44 Example: 'Divine music! It causes all prejudices to fall away, all the annoyances born of some earlier work where Orpheus had ventured to break his lyre, etc.' All this to suggest no doubt that Mauriac's new *Memoirs* are better than the old ones. (J. Piatier, *Le Monde*, 6 Nov. 1965.)

from foreign worlds, hence suspect. We have here a conservative decision to change nothing in the way that different kinds of vocabulary are marked off and shared out: it is as though language were a kind of gold rush, in which each discipline (a concept which in fact derives from the way universities organize their work) is conceded a small language territory, a sort of terminological miner's claim whose confines one cannot leave (philosophy, for example, is allowed its own jargon). The territory conceded to criticism is, however, bizarre: it is particular, since foreign words cannot be introduced into it (as if criticism had extremely small conceptual needs), yet it is nevertheless promoted to the dignity of a universal language. This universality, which is nothing but *current usage*, is faked: made up from an enormous quantity of tics and refusals, it is nothing more than yet another particular language: it is universality appropriated by the class of property owners.

You can describe this linguistic narcissim in another way: 'jargon' is the language which the Other uses; the Other (and not Others) is that which is not yourself; this is why we find another's way of speaking painful. As soon as a language is no longer that of our own community we judge it to be useless, empty, raving,[45] used for reasons which are not serious but trivial and base (snobbery, complacency): thus the language of 'neo-criticism' seems to

45 M. de Norpois, eponymous figure of old criticism, says of Bergotte's language: 'This misconception which consists of stringing along highly impressive-sounding words and only afterwards worrying about their meaning' (M. Proust, *A la recherche du temps perdu*, Pléaide, I, p.474).

'archeo-criticism' as strange as Yiddish (a suspect comparison in any event),[46] to which one could reply that Yiddish *too* can be learnt.[47] *Why not say things more simply*? How many times have we heard that phrase? But how many times would we be justified in throwing it back? Even leaving aside the healthily and joyously esoteric character of some plebeian language,[48] is old criticism so sure that it too does not have its own gratuitous floweriness? If I myself were an old critic, wouldn't I have some reason to ask my colleagues to write *Mr Piroué writes French well* rather than: *We must praise the pen of Mr Piroué for stimulating us frequently with the unexpectedness and the felicity of his expressions*, or again to describe modestly as 'indignation' *the whole of that stirring of the heart which warms the pen and loads it with murderous sharp tips.*[49] What are we to make of this writer's pen which one heats, which sometimes excites agreeably and sometimes murders? In truth, this language is clear only to the extent that it is generally accepted.

In fact, the literary language of old criticism is a matter of indifference to us. We know that old criticism cannot write in any other way unless it begins to think in some

---

46 R.M. Albérès, *Arts* 15 Dec. 1965 (Survey of criticism). The language of newspapers and the University is, it appears, not part of this Yiddish. Mr Albérès is a journalist and a university teacher.

47 At the Ecole Nationale des Langues Orientales.

48 'Work programme for the Tricolores [French rugby team]: structure the pack, develop our heeling technique, re-examine the problem of the throw-in' (*L'Equipe*, 1 Dec. 1965).

49 P.H. Simon, *Le Monde*, 1 Dec. 1965, and J. Piatier, *Le Monde*, 23 Oct. 1965.

other way. For to write is *already* to organize the world, it is *already* to think (to learn a language is to learn how one thinks in that language). It is thus useless (though critical verisimilitude persists in expecting it) to ask the Other to re-write himself if he has not decided to re-think himself. You see in the jargon of new criticism nothing but extravagances of form stuck on top of a content of platitudes: it is indeed possible to 'reduce' a language by abolishing the system that makes it up, that is to say the links which give meaning to the words: in this way one can translate anything into the matter-of-fact style of Molière's character Chrysale:* why not reduce the Freudian 'super-ego' to the 'moral conscience' of classical psychology? *What! Is that all it is?* Yes, if one abolishes all the rest. In literature, rewriting in a psychoanalytical sense does not exist because the writer does not have a pre-language from which he could choose an expression among a number of standardized codes (which is not to say that he does not have to try tirelessly to do so). There is clarity in writing, but this clarity has more to do with the *Nuit de l'encrier* of which Mallarmé* spoke than with modern pastiches of Voltaire or Nisard. Clarity is not an attribute of writing, it is writing itself, from the very moment at which it becomes writing, it is the happiness of writing, it is all the desire which is writing. Certainly the problem of the limits of his reception is a very serious one for a writer; but at least he chooses those limits, and if it happens that he accepts narrow limits, it is precisely because to write is not to enter into an easy relationship with an *average* of all possible readers, it is to enter into a difficult relationship with our own language: a writer has greater obligations towards a way of speaking which is the truth for him than towards the critic of the *Nation française* or *Le Monde*. 'Jargon' is not an instrument of apearances, as has been suggested with gratuitous malevolence;[50] 'jargon' is a way of imagining (and shocks as imagination does), a way of approaching metaphorical language which intellectual discourse will need one day.

I am here defending the right to language, not my own 'jargon'. In any event how could I speak about my own jargon? There is a disturbing problem (a problem of identity) involved in imagining that one could be the owner of a certain kind of utterance, that it is necessary to defend its nature as if it were a possession. Do I then exist *before* my language? Who might this *I* be, owner of precisely that which causes me to exist? How can I live my language as a simple attribute of my person? How can one believe that if I speak, it is because I am? Outside of literature, it is perhaps possible to entertain these illusions; but literature is precisely what stops us from doing so. The prohibition which you cast upon other forms of language is simply a way of excluding yourselves from literature: one can no longer, one should no longer be able to, as Saint-Marc Girardin[51]* did in his time, act as a policeman towards art and at the same time claim to talk about it.

A-symbolia

Critical verisimilitude is thus in 1965: one must talk of a book with '*objectivity*', '*good taste*' and '*clarity*'. Those

50 Picard, p.52.

51 Warning youth against '*the moral illusions and confusions*' spread by the '*books of the time*'.

rules do not belong to our time: the last two come from the classical (seventeenth) century and the first from the positivist (nineteenth) century. Thus is made up a body of diffuse norms, half-aesthetic (from the classical notion of Beauty), half-reasonable (from 'common sense'): a sort of reassuring turnstile is established connecting art and science, which allows people never to be completely in one field or the other.

This ambiguity is expressed in one more proposition which seems to be the last will and testament of old criticism, so religiously is it held to, namely that we must respect the '*specificity*' of literature.[52] Set up like a small weapon of war against new criticism, which is accused of being indifferent '*to what is literary in literature*' and of destroying '*literature as a primary reality*',[53] endlessly repeated but never explained, this proposition has obviously the unattackable virtue of a tautology: *literature is literature*; one can thus at one and the same time become indignant at the ingratitude of new criticism for being unaware that literature, by decree of verisimilitude, comprises Art, Emotion, Beauty, Humanity,[54] and pretend to call upon criticism to become a new science, which would at last consider the literary object 'in itself', without ever again owing anything to historical or anthropological sciences; this 'renewal' is in any event rather stale: in more or less the same terms Brunetière* reproached Taine* with having neglected the 'essence of literature', that is to say 'the laws specific to the genre'.

52 Picard, p.117.

53 Picard, pp.104,122.

54 'The abstraction of this new criticism, inhuman and anti-literary' (*Revue parlementaire*, 15 Nov. 1965).

To attempt to establish the structure of literary works is an important task and some researchers devote much time to it, using methods, it is true, of which old criticism says nothing. This is completely to be expected, since old criticism claims to find structures without, however, practising 'structuralism' (a word which annoys it and of which we should 'cleanse' the French language). It is true that reading a work should be done at the level of the work; but on the one hand, one cannot see how, once the forms have been laid down, one could avoid finding content, which comes from history or the *psyche*, in short from that '*elsewhere*' which old criticism refuses to have anything to do with; and on the other hand, the structural analysis of works is much harder work than people think, for if it is not an amiable chat about the plan of the work, it can only be done as a function of logical models: in fact, the specificity of literature can only be postulated within a general theory of signs: in order to have the right to defend an immanent reading of the work, one must know about logic, history, psychoanalysis; in sum, to return the work to literature one must go outside literature and draw on anthropological knowledge. One can doubt that old criticism is ready to do that. It seems that for it, a purely aesthetic specificity is to be defended: it wants to protect in the work an absolute value, untouched by any of those unworthy '*outside*' things which history and the depths of the *psyche* are: what it wants is not a work made from something but a *pure* work, which is shielded from all compromise with the world, all misalliance with desire. The model of this chaste structuralism is quite simply moral.

'*On the subject of the gods*', recommended Demetrius Phalereus,* '*say that they are gods.*' The final imperative of critical verisimilitude is of the same kind: *on the subject of literature, say that it is literature*. This tautology is not gratuitous: at first, they pretend to believe that it is possible to talk of literature and to make it the *object* of discourse; but this discourse leads nowhere, since it has nothing to say of this object other than that it is itself. Critical verisimilitude leads indeed to silence or its substitute, idle talk: an amiable *chat*, as Roman Jakobson* was already saying aby 1921 of the history of literature. Paralysed by the prohibitions which accompany its 'respect' for the work (which is for it nothing but the exclusive perception of literal meaning), critical verisimilitude is almost reduced to silence: the thin slice of language which all this censure leaves it allows it only to claim the rights that institutions have over dead writers. It has deprived itself of the capacity to add a second discourse to the work, because it does not accept the accompanying risks.

After all, silence is a way of taking one's leave. Let us then, as a kind of farewell, point out the failure of this criticism. Since its object is literature, it might have sought to establish the conditions under which a work is possible, to sketch out if not a science, at least a technique of the literary operation; but it is to the writers themselves that it has left the task – and the trouble – of undertaking this enquiry (and luckily, from Mallarmé to Blanchot,* they have not avoided it): *they* have never failed to recognize that language is the very stuff of literature, thus moving forward, in their own way, towards the *objective* truth of their art. At least they might have agreed to free criticism – which is not science and does not claim to be science – so that it might tell us the meaning that people of our own time can give to works from the past. Do they believe that Racine 'in itself', taking the text literally, has any connection with us? Seriously, of what concern can '*violent yet chaste*' drama be to us? What can it mean today to talk of a '*proud and generous prince*'?[55] What unusual language! They speak of a '*virile*' hero (without however allowing anyone ever to allude to his sexual organ); carried over into some parody, such an expression would make people laugh; and that is just what happens anyway when we read it, in the 'Letter from Sophocles to Racine', which Gisèle, Albertine's friend, has written for a school exam ('*the characters are virile*').[56] Besides, what were Gisèle and Andrée doing if not engaging in old criticism when, in relation to the same Racine, they spoke of the 'tragic genre', of the 'plot' (we find once again the '*laws of genre*'), 'well-delineated personalities' (here we have '*the coherence of the psychological implications*'), remarking that *Athalie* is not a 'tragedy of love' (in the same way, we are reminded that *Andromaque* is not a patriotic play), etc.?[57] The critical vocabulary in whose name we are brought to task is that of a young girl who was sitting a school certificate examination three quarters of a century ago. Since, then, however, there have been Marx, Freud, Nietzsche. Elsewhere, Lucien Febvre* and Merleau-Ponty* have claimed the right to *rewrite* endlessly the history of history and the history of philosophy so that an object from the past is

55 Picard, pp.34,32.

56 M. Proust, *A la recherche du temps perdu*, Pléiade, I, p.912.

57 Picard, p.30. I have quite obviously never made out *Andromaque* to be a patriotic drama; such distinctions of genre were not my aim – which is exactly what I was criticized for. I spoke about the figure of the Father in *Andromaque* and that is all.

always a total object. Why is no such voice raised to guarantee the same right to literature?

This silence and this failure can be expressed, if not explained, in another way. The old critic is the victim of a condition which language analysts are familiar with called *a-symbolia*:[58] he cannot perceive or manipulate symbols, that is, co-existence of meaning; for him, the very general symbolic function which, as soon as one goes beyond narrowly rational uses of language, allows people to construct ideas, images and works of art, is disturbed, limited or censored.

It is certainly possible to speak of a work of literature without making any reference to symbols. That depends on the point of view one chooses and one only has to declare it. Leaving aside the enormous area of established literary practice which is really part of history,[59] and confining ourselves to the particular work, it is certain that if I am looking at *Andromaque* from the point of view of the takings at the door or at Proust's manuscripts from the point of view of the physical nature of his corrections to the manuscript, it is hardly necessary to believe or disbelieve in the symbolic nature of literary works: an aphasic patient can perfectly well weave baskets or do carpentry. But as soon as one claims to examine the work in itself, from the point of view of its make-up, it becomes impossible not to raise broad questions of symbolic meaning.

---

58 H. Hécaen and R. Angelergues, *Pathologie du langage*, Larousse, 1965, p.32.
59 Cf. *Sur Racine*, 'History or Literature?' Seuil 1963, pp.147 ff.

And that is what new criticism has done. Everyone knows that it has openly worked, up until now, by taking as its starting-point the symbolic nature of works and what Bachelard* called the point where the image fails. However, in the quarrel which old criticism has picked with new criticism, nobody seemed to think for a minute that symbols entered into the question and that as a consequence it was necessary to discuss the freedoms and the limits of an explicitly symbolic criticism: people have endowed literal readings with totalitarian rights, without ever suggesting that the symbol might have some rights which are perhaps not just whatever residual freedoms a literal reading chooses not to lay claim to. Does the letter exclude the symbol or does it on the contrary make the symbol possible? Does the work have meaning literally or else symbolically – or again, in Rimbaud's phrase, '*literally and in every sense*'?[60] This could be what is at stake in the debate. The analyses of *On Racine* all derive from a certain logic of symbols, as the preface of the book declared. It was necessary either to contest overall the existence or the possibility of this logic (which would have had the advantage, as they say, of '*raising the tone of the debate*'), or else to show that the author of *On Racine* had applied the rules of that logic badly – which he would have freely allowed, especially two years after having published his book and six years after having written it. Contesting all the details of a book without ever giving any indication that one has perceived its overall thrust, that is to say quite simply, its meaning, is indeed a strange

60 Rimbaud to his mother, who did not understand *Une Saison en Enfer*: 'I meant to say what it says, literally and in every sense' (*Oeuvres complètes*, Pléiade, p.656).

lesson in how to read. Old criticism reminds one of those 'primitive' people described by Ombredane who, upon seeing a film for the first time in their lives, take in from the scene nothing but a hen which is crossing the village square. It is not reasonable to accord absolute dominion to the letter of a text and then afterwards, without warning, to contest each symbol in the name of an inappropriate principle. Would you blame a Chinese (since new criticism seems to you to be a strange language) for the mistakes he is making in French *when he is talking Chinese*?

But why, after all, this deafness to symbols, this *a-symbolia*? What is so threatening in a symbol? Multiple meaning is the basis of a book; why then does it endanger the discourse which is applied to the book? And why, once again, today?

II

Nothing is more essential to a society than the *classification* of its languages. To change this classification, to relocate discourse, is to bring about a revolution. For two centuries, French classicism was defined by the separation, the hierarchy and the stability of its modes of writing, and the romantic revolution presented itself as a disturbance in the way writing was conceived. However, for nearly a hundred years, since Mallarmé no doubt, an important reworking of the locus of our literature has been taking place: an exchange, an interpenetration, a unification has been occurring as regards the poetic and the critical functions of writing;[61] not only do the writers themselves practise criticism, but their work, often, articulates the conditions of its own birth (Proust) or even of its own absence (Blanchot); the same language tends to circulate everywhere in literature and even behind itself; the book is often approached from the other side by the person writing it; there are no longer either poets or

---

61 Gérard Genette "Rhétorique et enseignement" ["Rhetoric and teaching"], *Figures II*, Paris, Editions du Seuil, 1969, pp. 23–42.

novelists: there is no longer anything but writing.[62]

The crisis of commentary

And so it is that the critic, in a complementary movement, becomes a writer in his turn. Naturally, wanting to be a writer is not an aspiration to acquire a particular status, but a wish to exist in a particular way. What do we care whether it is more glorious to be a novelist, a poet, an essayist or a chronicler? The writer cannot be defined in terms of his role or his value but only by a certain *awareness of discourse*. A writer is someone for whom language constitutes a problem, who is aware of the depth of language, not its instrumentality or its beauty. Books of criticism are thus born, offering themselves to be read in the same manner as the strictly literary work, although the status of their authors is that of critic and not writer. If new criticism has any reality, it is there: not in the unity of its methods and even less in the snobbery which, it is so comfortably asserted, supports it, but in the solitude of the act of criticism, which is now declared to be a complete act of writing, far removed from the excuses of science or institutions. Formerly separated by the worn-out myth of the '*superb creator and the humble servant, both necessary, each in his place*, etc.', the writer and the critic come together, working on the same difficult tasks and faced with the same object: language.

62 'Poetry, novels, short stories are remarkable antiquities which no longer fool anyone, or hardly anyone. Poems, narratives – what's the use of them? There is nothing but writing left.' J.M.G. Le Clézio (foreword to *La Fièvre*, Paris, Gallimard, 1965.)

We have seen that this last transgression has not been happily accepted. And yet, although it is still necessary to do battle on behalf of this transgression, it has perhaps already been overtaken by another re-working which is appearing on the horizon: it is not only criticism which is starting out on this 'journey across writing',[63] which will perhaps leave its mark on our century, it is intellectual discourse as a whole. It is now four centuries since Ignatius Loyola,the founder of the order which has done the most for rhetoric, left in his *Spiritual Exercises* the model of a dramatized discourse which has been subject to an influence other than that of syllogism or abstraction, as Georges Bataille* in his perspicacity did not fail to bring to our attention.[64] Since then, through the influence of writers such as Sade and Nietzsche, the rules of intellectual presentation are periodically by-passed and also, as it were, consigned to the flames. It is that, apparently, which is at issue today. Intellect is acceding to another logic, it is approaching the naked region of 'internal experience': one and the same truth, common to all discourse, is being sought, whether the work be fictional, poetic or discursive, because henceforth this truth is that of discourse itself. When Jacques Lacan speaks,[65] he sub-

---

63 Philippe Sollers*, 'Dante et la traversée de l'écriture', *Tel Quel*, 23, Autumn 1965.

64 'At this point, we see the secondary meaning of the word to dramatize: it is the desire, grafted on to the text, not to be limited to what has been stated, to oblige the reader to feel the chill of the wind, to be naked... In this connection, it is a classic error to view the Exercises of St Ignatius as belonging to discursive method' (*L'expérience intérieure*, Gallimard, 1954, p.26).

65 At his seminar at the Ecole pratique des Hautes Etudes.

stitutes for the traditional abstraction of concepts a total expansion of the image in the field of discourse, so that it no longer separates the particular case from the idea, and is itself truth. In another way, breaking free from the ordinary notion of 'development', Claude Lévi-Strauss's* *Le Cru et le cuit (1964)* offers a new rhetoric of *variation* and thus encourages us to take a certain responsibility for form, something one does not often find in works on the social sciences. A transformation of discursive writing is no doubt in progress, the same transformation in fact which brings the critic closer to the writer: we are entering a *general crisis of commentary,* perhaps as important as that which marked, in relation to the same problem, the transition from the Middle Ages to the Renaissance.

This crisis is indeed inevitable as soon as one discovers – or rediscovers – the symbolic nature of language, or, if one prefers, the linguistic nature of the symbol. That is what is happening today under the combined influence of psychoanalysis and structuralism. For a long period, classico-bourgeois society saw in discourse an instrument or a decoration; nowadays we see in it a sign and a truth. Everything which is affected by language is thus in a certain way called into question: philosophy, social sciences, literature.

Here is doubtless the debate into which we must bring back literary criticism; here is (at least partly) what is at stake when we practise literary criticism. What is the relationship between the work and language? If the work is symbolic, by what rules of reading is one bound? Can there be a science of written symbols? Can the language of the critic itself be symbolic?

Part II

Plural language

As a genre, the diary has been treated in two very different ways by the sociologist Alain Girard* and the writer Maurice Blanchot.[66] For the one, the diary is the expression of a certain number of social, family, professional (and so on) circumstances; for the other, it is an anguished way of delaying the fatal solitude of writing. The diary thus has at least two meanings and each is plausible because it is coherent.

That is an everyday fact, a thousand examples of which are to be found in the history of criticism and in the variety of readings to which the same work can give rise: facts at least bear witness to the truth that the work has several meanings. Each age can indeed believe that it holds the canonical meaning of the work, but it suffices to have a slightly broader historical perspective in order for this singular meaning to be transformed into a plural meaning and the closed work to be transformed into an open work.[67] The very definition of the work is changing: it is no longer a historical fact, it is becoming an anthropological fact, since no history can exhaust its meaning. The variety of meanings is not a matter of a relativist approach to human mores; it designates not the tendency that society has to err but a disposition towards openness; the work holds several meanings simultaneously, by its very structure, and not as a result of some infirmity in those who read it. Therein lies its symbolic

---

66 Alain Girard, *Le Journal intime*, PUF, 1963; Maurice Blanchot, *L'Espace littéraire*, Gallimard, 1955, p.20.
67 See Umberto Eco, *L'Oeuvre Ouverte*, Seuil, 1965.

nature: the symbol is not the image but the very plurality of meanings.[68]

The symbol is constant. The only things which can change are the awareness society has of it and the rights society gives to it. The freedom of the symbol was recognized and to some extent encoded in the Middle Ages, as can be seen in the theory of the four meanings;[69] on the other hand, it was accepted only with difficulty by classical society, which was unaware of it, or, as happens today, censured it. The history of the freedom of the symbol has

---

68 I am not unaware that the word *symbol* has quite a different meaning in semiology, where symbolic systems are on the contrary those in which 'a single form can be constructed, and a unit of content has a one-to-one correspondence with each unit of expression', in contrast with semiotic systems (language, dream) in which it is necessary to 'postulate two different forms, one for the expression, the other for the content, without any correspondence between them' (N. Ruwet, 'La Linguistique générale aujourd'hui' *Archives européennes de Sociologie*, V, 1964, p.287.

It is clear that according to that definition, the symbols of the work belong to a semiotic and not a symbolic order. However, I am provisionally keeping here the word *symbol*, with the general meaning which P. Ricoeur gives it which is sufficient for the remarks which follow. ('Symbol exists when language produces signs of a compound order where the meaning, not content to designate something, designates another meaning which could not be reached except by and through what is intended by it', *De l'Interprétation, essai sur Freud,* Seuil, 1965, p.25.)

69 Literal, allegorical, moral and anagogical meanings. There also exists obviously a journey across meanings which is guided towards the anagogical meaning.

often been a violent one, and naturally this fact also has its own meaning: one cannot censure symbols with impunity. However that may be, that particular problem is an institutional one and not, so to speak, structural: whatever societies think or decree, the work goes beyond them, travels through them, in the manner of a form which is filled turn and turn about by more or less contingent and historical meanings: a work is 'eternal' not because it imposes a single meaning on different men, but because it suggests different meanings to one man, who always speaks the same symbolic language across many periods of time: the work proposes, man disposes.

Every reader knows that, if he is prepared not to let himself be intimidated by the censorship implicit in literal readings: does he not feel that he is re-entering into contact with a certain *beyond* of the text, as if the primary language of the work gave rise within him to other words and taught him to speak a second language? That is what is called *dreaming*. But the dream has its pathways, as Bachelard said, and those are the pathways which are marked out before an utterance by the second language of the work. Literature is the exploration of names: Proust extracted a whole world from these few sounds: *Guermantes*.* Fundamentally, the writer always nurtures the belief that signs are not arbitrary and that the name is a natural property of the thing: writers are followers of Cratylus and not of Hermogenes. So, *we should read as people write*: thus do we 'glorify' literature (to glorify is 'to show a thing in its essence'); for if words had only one meaning, the dictionary meaning, and if a second language did not appear, disturbing and liberating 'the certainties of language', there would be no literature.[70] That is why the rules of reading are not those of literalness but those of allusion: they are linguistic rules, not philological rules.[71]

Philology does indeed have the task of fixing the literal meaning of an utterance, but it has no hold on second meanings. On the contrary, the work of linguistics is not to reduce the ambiguities of language but to comprehend them and, so to speak, to *institute* them. What poets have long known by the name of *suggestion* or *evocation* the linguist is beginning to approach, thus giving a scientific status to floating meanings. R. Jakobson has insisted on the constitutive ambiguity of the poetic (literary) message; that is to say that this ambiguity is not a matter of an aesthetic opinion on the 'freedoms' of interpretation and even less of a moral censure of the risks of interpretation, but it does mean that this ambiguity can be formulated in terms of a code: the symbolic language to which

---

70 Mallarmé: 'If I follow you,' he writes to Francis Vielé-Griffin, 'you are making the creative privilege of the poet depend on the imperfection of the instrument which he must play; a language hypothetically adequate for translating his thought would dispense with the man of letters, whose name as a result would be Mr Everyman.' (Quoted by J.–P. Richard, *L'Univers imaginaire de Mallarmé*, Seuil, 1961, p.576.)

71 Several times recently new criticism has been reproached with frustrating the work of the educator, which is essentially, it seems, to *teach people to read*. The rhetoric of the ancients aimed for its part to *teach people to write*: it gave rules for creation (imitation) not for reception. One can indeed wonder whether reading is not diminished by thus isolating its rules. To read well is virtually to write well, that is to say to write according to symbol.

literary works belong is *by its very structure* a plural language whose code is constructed in such a way that every utterance (every work) engendered by it has multiple meanings. This tendency already exists in language proper which contains many more uncertainties than people are prepared to admit – linguists are now beginning to work on that.[72] However, the ambiguities of practical language are nothing compared with those of literary language. The former are in fact reducible by virtue of the *situation* in which they appear: something outside the most ambiguous sentence – a context, a gesture, a memory – tells us how to understand it if we want to make *practical* use of the information it has the task of conveying: circumstances create a clear meaning.

Nothing of the sort applies in the case of the work of literature: for us the work has no set of contingent circumstances, and therein lies, perhaps, the best definition of it: the work is not surrounded, designated, protected or directed by any situation, no practical life is there to tell us the meaning which should be given to it; there is always something quotation-like about it: its ambiguity is absolutely pure: no matter how prolix it is, it always has something of Pythian concision, utterances which are in accordance with a primary code (the Pythoness did not divagate) and yet open to several meanings, for the utterances were made independently of any *situation* – unless it were the very situation of ambiguity itself: the work is always in a prophetic situation. It is true that by adding *my* situation to my reading of a work I can reduce its

72 Cf. A.J. Greimas, *Cours de Sémantique*, particularly chapter VI on the isotopy of discourse (roneoed course-notes from the Ecole normale supérieure de Saint-Cloud, 1964).

ambiguity (and that is what usually happens); but this situation, as it changes, *composes* the work and does not rediscover it: as soon as I submit to the constraints of the symbolic code on which it is based, that is to say as soon as I agree to inscribe my reading in the symbolic domain, the work cannot protest against the meaning I give it, but neither can the work authenticate that meaning, for the second code of the work is limiting, not prescriptive: it marks out volumes of meaning, not lines of meaning; it sets up ambiguities, not a meaning.

Since it is abstracted from any *situation*, the work by that very fact offers itself for exploration: it becomes, to the person who writes or reads it, a question which is put to language, the foundations of which are experienced and the limits of which are being reached. The work thus makes itself the repository of a vast unceasing investigation into words.[73] It is always claimed that the symbol is only a property of imagination. The symbol also has a critical function, and the object of its criticism is language itself. To the *Critiques of Reason* which philosophy has given us we can add today a *Critique of Language* which is literature itself.

Now if it is true that the work by its very structure contains a multiple meaning, it must give rise to two different discourses: for one can on the one hand try to read all the meanings the work covers or, what amounts to the same thing, the empty meaning which underlies them all; and one can on the other hand single out only one of them. In no case ought these two discourses to be confused with

73 The writer's investigations into language: this theme was isolated and examined by Marthe Robert in relation to Kafka (especially in *Kafka*, Gallimard, 'Bibliothèque idéale', 1960).

one another, for they are not directed at the same object nor are they controlled by the same sanctions. One can propose to give the name *science of literature* (or of writing) to that general discourse whose object is not a particular meaning but the very plurality of the meanings of the work, and to give the name *literary criticism* to that other discourse which openly and at its peril adopts the intention of giving a particular meaning to the work. This distinction is, however, not sufficient. As the giving of meaning can be written or silent we shall separate the *reading* of the work from *criticism* of it: the first is immediate; the second is mediated by an intermediary language, which is the writing of the critic. *Science*, *Criticism*, *Reading* – these are the three kinds of discourse we must traverse in order to weave around the work its garland of language.

The science of literature

We have a history of literature but not a science of literature, no doubt because we have not yet been able fully to recognize the nature of the literary *object*, which is a written object. As soon as one is prepared to allow (and to draw the consequences of the fact) that the work is made from writing, a *certain kind* of literary science is possible. If this science should come into existence one day, its object could not be to impose a meaning on the work, in the name of which it would arrogate to itself the right to reject other meanings: in so doing it would compromise itself (just as it has done up till now). It cannot be a science of the content of works (over which only the most rigorous historical science can have a hold), but a science of the *conditions* of content, that is to say of forms: it will concern itself with the variations of the meanings engendered and, so to speak, *engenderable* by works: it will not interpret symbols but only their polyvalence; in a word, its object will no longer be the full meanings of the work but on the contrary the empty meaning which underpins them all.

Its model will obviously be linguistic. Faced with the impossibility of mastering all the sentences of a language, the linguist is satisfied to establish a *hypothetical model of description* which allows him to explain how the infinity of sentences in a language is generated.[74] Whatever corrections one might be led to make, there is no reason not to try to apply such a method to works of literature: these works are themselves like immense 'sentences' derived from the general language of symbols through a certain number of set transformations or in a more general way through a certain logic of meaning which will have to be described. In other words linguistics can give to literature the generative model which is the underlying principle of all sciences, since there must always be certain rules to explain certain results. The science of literature will thus have as its object of investigation not the reason why such and such a meaning must be accepted nor even why it was accepted (that, once again, is a matter for the historian), but rather the reason why it is *acceptable*, not at all as a function of philological rules of literalness but as a function of linguistic rules concerning symbols. Here we find again, transposed to the level of a science of discourse, the task undertaken by recent linguistics, which is to describe the *grammaticality* of sen-

74 Here I am thinking, obviously, of the work of N. Chomsky and of the propositions of transformational grammar.

tences, not their meaning. In the same way, we shall try to describe the *acceptability* of works, not their meaning. We shall not classify the whole set of possible meanings as belonging to an immutable order of things but rather as being the traces of an immense 'operative' tendency (since it allows people to write works), extended beyond the author to society. Corresponding to the *language faculty* postulated by Humboldt* and Chomsky*, there is perhaps in people a *literature faculty*, an energy of discourse, which has nothing to do with 'genius', for it is made up not of inspiration or personal will-power but of rules built up by many people besides the author. It is not images, ideas or lines of verse which the mythical voice of the Muse breathes into the writer, it is the great logic of symbols and great empty forms which allow him to speak and to operate.

One can imagine the sacrifices which such a science would impose on those things that we love or believe we love in literature when we talk about it, that is to say, in many cases, *the author*. And yet: how could science speak of *one* author? The science of literature can only link the literary work to myth, although the literary work is signed and myth is not.[75] We are generally inclined, at least today, to believe that the author can lay claim to the meaning of his work and can himself make that its legal meaning; from this notion flows the unreasonable interrogation directed by the critic at the dead writer, at his life, at the traces of his intentions, so that he himself can

---

75 'The myth is discourse which seems not to have any true emitter who would be responsible for the content and claim the meaning: it is thus enigmatic' (L. Sebag, 'Le Mythe: Code et Message', *Temps modernes*, March 1965).

guarantee the meaning of his work: people want at all costs to make the dead person, or a substitute for him, speak. Such substitutes may be his historical period, the genre, the vocabulary, in a word everything that is *contemporary* with the author; these contemporary phenomena acquire metonymically the author's right over his creation. Even more: we are asked to wait until the author is dead so that we can treat him with 'objectivity'[§]; a strange reversal indeed: it is at the very moment when the work becomes mythical that we are supposed to regard it as a precise phenomenon.

Death has another significance: it renders unreal the author's signature and transforms the work into myth: the truth contained in anecdotes completely fails to catch up with the truth embodied in the symbols.[76] Popular sentiment is well aware of the fact: we do not go to see 'a work of Racine's' performed but rather 'Racine', in much the same way as one would go to see 'a Western', as if we lifted out, as our fancy took us, at a particular moment of our week, a bit of the substance of a great myth in order to take sustenance from it; we don't go to see *Phèdre* but 'La Berma* in *Phèdre*, just as we would read Sophocles,

---

[§] Translator's note: This is doubtless a reference to the fact that at the time Barthes was writing *Criticism and Truth* the custom still prevailed at the Sorbonne of not allowing people to present theses on authors who were still alive!

76 'What causes posterity's judgment on the individual to be more correct than that of contemporaries lies within death. One develops in one's own way only after one's death...' (F. Kafka, *Préparatifs de noce à la campagne*, Gallimard, 1957, p.366).

Freud, Hölderlin and Kierkegaard in *Oedipus Rex* and *Antigone*. And we are right, for we refuse thus to allow the dead to hold the living in their grip, we free the work from the constraints of intention, we rediscover the mythological trembling of meanings. By erasing the author's signature, death founds the truth of the work, which is enigma. No doubt a 'civilized' work cannot be treated as a myth in the ethnological meaning of the term; but the difference stems less from the signature of the message than from its substance: our works are written, which imposes constraints on them unknown to the oral myth: it is a mythology of writing which awaits us; its object will be not *determinate* works, that is to say works placed in a process of determination of which one person (the author) would be the origin, but rather works *traversed* by that great mythical writing in which humanity tries out its meanings, that is to say its desires.

We must then decide to rearrange the objects of literary science. The author and the work are only the starting-points of an analysis whose horizon is a language: there cannot be a science of Dante, Shakespeare or Racine but only a science of discourse. This science will have two important areas, according to the signs it is dealing with; the first area will include those signs which are shorter than the sentence, such as the figures of antiquity, phenomena of connotation, 'semantic anomalies',[77] etc., in a word all of the characteristics of literary language as a whole; the second area will deal with signs which are longer than the sentence, those parts of discourse from which one can infer a structure of the narrative, of the

---

77 T. Todorov, 'Les anomalies sémantiques', *Langages*, I, 1966, pp.100–123.

poetic message, of the discursive text,[78] etc. Large and small units of discourse obviously exist in a relationship of integration (like phonemes in relation to words and words in relation to the sentence), but they are made up of levels which exist independently of description. Considered in this way, the literary text will offer itself up to analyses which are *certain*, but it is obvious that these analyses will leave an enormous residue beyond their reach. This residue will correspond pretty well to what today we judge to be essential in the work (personal genuis, art, humanity), unless we rediscover an interest in and love for the truth of myths.

The objectivity required by this new science of literature will no longer relate to the immediate work (which is a matter for literary history or philology) but to its intelligibility. Just as phonology, without rejecting the experimental verification of phonetics, has set up a new objectivity for phonic meaning (no longer only for physical sound), so also there is an objectivity of the symbol which is different from that necessary for the establishment of

---

78 The structural analysis of narrative is currently the subject of preliminary research, being carried out in particular at the Centre d'Etudes des Communications de Masse at the Ecole pratique des Hautes Etudes, building on the work of V. Propp and C. Lévi-Strauss. On the poetic message, see R. Jakobson, *Essais de Linguistique générale*, Minuit, 1963, ch. II, and Nicolás Ruwet: 'L'analyse structurale de la poésie', *Linguistics*, 2, Dec. 1963 and 'Analyse structurale d'un poème français', *Linguistics*, 3, Jan. 1964. Cf. also: C. Lévi-Strauss and R. Jakobson: 'Les Chats de Charles Baudelaire', *L'Homme*, II, 1962, p.2 and Jean Cohen, *Structure du langage poétique*, Flammarion, 1966.

literal meaning. The object furnishes substantial constraints and not rules of meaning: the 'grammar' of the work is not that of the idiom in which it is written, and the objectivity of the new science depends on this second grammar, not on the first. What will concern the science of literature is not that the work happens to have existed, it is the fact that it happens to have been and is still understood: the intelligible will be the source of its 'objectivity'.

It will thus be necessary to bid farewell to the idea that the science of literature can teach us the meaning to be attributed infallibly to a work: it will neither *give* nor even *rediscover* any meaning, but it will describe according to which logic it is that meanings are engendered in a manner which is capable of being *accepted* by the symbolic logic of humankind, just as sentences in French are *accepted* by the 'linguistic feeling' of the French. No doubt a long road remains to be travelled before we shall have at our disposal a linguistics of discourse, that is to say a true science of literature in conformity with the verbal nature of its object. For if linguistics can help us, it alone cannot resolve the problems presented by those new objects which are the parts of speech and double meanings. In particular it will need the help of history, which will inform it of how long, often how very long, secondary codes (such as the code of rhetoric) can last, as well as the help of anthropology, which will allow us, by means of successive comparisons and integrations, to describe the general logic of signifiers.

Criticism

Criticism is not science. Science deals with meanings, criticism produces them. It occupies, as has been said, an intermediate position between science and reading; it gives a language to the particular discourse [*pure parole*] which reads literature and gives one voice [*une parole*] (among others) to the mythical language [*langue*] of which the work is made and with which science is concerned.

The relationship of criticism to the work is that of a meaning to a form. The critic cannot claim to 'translate' the work, and particularly not to make it clearer, for nothing is clearer than the work. What the critic can do is to 'engender' a certain meaning by deriving it from the form which is the work. If he reads 'the daughter of Minos and Pasiphaë', his role is not to establish that we are dealing with Phaedra (the philologists will do that very well), but rather to conceive of a network of meanings such that the chthonic theme and the theme of the sun can take their place in the scheme according to certain logical requirements to which we shall return in a moment. The critic separates meanings, he causes a second language – that is to say, a coherence of signs – to float above the first language of the work. In brief, we are concerned with a kind of anamorphosis, given of course that on the one hand the work never lends itself to a pure reflection (it is not a specular object like an apple or a box), and on the other hand that the anamorphosis itself is a *guided* transformation, subject to optical constraints: out of what it reflects, it must transform *everything*; transform only according to certain laws; transform always in the same direction. Those are the three constraints which limit criticism.

The critic cannot say '*just anything at all*'.[79] What con-

---

79 Accusation directed against new criticism by R. Picard, p.66.

strains his statements is not, however, the moral fear of 'delirium'; first of all because he leaves to others the unworthy task of arbitrarily dividing reason and unreason, in the very century in which the distinction between them is questioned;[80] secondly, because the right to 'speak deliriously' has been won by literature since Lautréamont* at least and because criticism could perfectly well enter a frenzy for poetic reasons, provided only that it declared its intentions; and finally because the delirious words of today are sometimes the truths of tomorrow: would not Taine appear 'delirious' to Boileau*, and Georges Blin* to Brunetière? No, if the critic is expected to say something (and not just anything at all), it is because he gives to words (the author's and his own) a signifying function and as a consequence the anamorphosis which he imprints on the work (and from which no one in the world can escape) is guided by the formal constraints of meaning: one does not create meaning in just any way (if you doubt that, try it): what controls the critic is not the meaning of the work, it is the meaning of what he says about it.

The first constraint is to consider that everything in the work has meaning: a grammar has not been properly described if *all* sentences cannot be explained with reference to it; a system of meaning is imperfect if *all* words cannot be fitted into an intelligible place: should there be one stroke too many then the description is not good. This rule of exhaustivity, which is well known to linguists, has a different scope from the kind of statistical

---

80 Is it necessary to recall that madness has a history – and that this history is not finished? (Michel Foucault*, *Folie et Déraison, Histoire de la Folie à l'âge classique*, Plon, 1961.)

controls which people seem to want to impose on the critic.[81] A stubborn opinion, whose source yet again is a supposed model derived from the physical sciences, whispers to him that he can take account only of frequent, repeated elements in the work, failing which he is guilty of '*unjustified generalizations*' and '*aberrant extrapolations*'; you cannot, he is told, treat as 'general' situations which one finds in only two or three tragedies of Racine. It must be repeated yet again[82] that, structurally, meaning is not born by repetition but by difference, so that a rare term, as soon as it is caught in a system of exclusions and relations, means just as much as a frequent term: the word *baobab* has neither more nor less meaning than the word *friend*. Counting units of meaning has its own interest and a part of linguistics is concerned with it; but it casts light on the *information* and not the meaning. From the standpoint of criticism, it can lead only to an impasse; for as soon as one defines the importance of a notation, or if one prefers, the degree of persuasion of an element, by the number of times it occurs, one must decide this number methodically: on the basis of what number of tragedies would I have the right to 'generalize' a Racinian situation? Five, six, ten? Must I go beyond the 'average' for the element to be noteworthy and for the meaning to burst forth? What shall I do with the rare terms? Get rid of them, calling them discreetly 'exceptions' or 'deviations'? That would be just creating absurdities which, precisely, semantics allows us to avoid. For

81 Picard, p.64.

82 Cf. Roland Barthes, 'A propos de deux ouvrages de Claude Lévi-Strauss: Sociologie et Socio-logique', *Informations sur les Sciences sociales*, Unesco, Dec. 1962, I, 4, p.116.

generalizing does not here designate a quantitative operation (inferring the truth of an element from the number of times it occurs) but a qualitative operation (inserting each term, even a rare one, in a general set of relations). It is quite true that one image alone does not make an imaginary world,[83] but an imaginary world cannot be described without this image, no matter how fragile or isolated it be, without the indestructible 'something' of this image. The '*generalizations*' of critical language are related to the scope of the relations of which a variant is part and not at all to the number of actual occurrences of the variant: a term may be formulated only once in the whole work and yet, as a result of a certain number of transformations which, precisely, define structural phenomena, be present in the work '*everywhere*' and '*always*'.[84]

These transformations also are subject to constraints: those of symbolic logic. People contrast the 'delirium' of new criticism with '*the elementary rules of scientific or even simply articulated thought*';[85] that is stupid; there exists a logic of the signifier. It is true that we are not well acquainted with it and it is not yet easy to know what kind of 'knowledge' it might be the object of; but at least one can approach it, as psychoanalysis and structuralism do; at least we know that one cannot talk about symbols in just any way at all; at least we can use – even if only provisionally – certain models which allow us to explain how chains of symbols are established along certain lines. These models ought to forewarn us against the surprise,

83 Picard, p.43.
84 Picard, p.19.
85 Picard, p.58.

itself quite surprising, that old criticism feels when it sees suffocation and poison, ice and fire brought together.[86] These forms of transformation have been articulated by both psychoanalysis and rhetoric.[87] They are, for example: substitution proper (metaphor), omission (ellipsis), condensation (homonymy), displacement (metonymy), denegation (antiphrasis). What the critic is seeking are transformations which are guided and not dependent on chance and also relate to very long chains (*bird*, *flight*, *flower*, *firework*, *fan*, *butterfly*, *ballerina* in Mallarmé)[88] giving rise to distant but licit connections (*the great calm river* and *the autumnal tree*), so that the work, far from being read in a 'delirious' way, is imbued with an ever-increasing unity. Are these connections facile? No more than those of poetry itself.

The book is a world. The critic experiences in relation to the book the same conditions governing discourse as the writer experiences in relation to the world. It is here that one reaches the third constraint limiting criticism. Like that of the writer, the anamorphosis imprinted by the critic on the object he is dealing with is always directed: it must proceed always in the same direction. What is that direction? Is it that of 'subjectivity', which has been claimed to be a tricky problem for the new critic? One usually understands by 'subjective' criticism a discourse left to the entire discretion of a *subject*, which takes no account at all of the *object*, and which one supposes (in order more effectively to attack it) to be nothing

86 Picard, pp.15,23.
87 Cf. E. Benveniste, 'Remarques sur la fonction du langage dans la découverte freudienne' *La Psychanalyse*, I, 1956, 3–39.
88 J.-P. Richard, pp.304 ff.

more than the anarchical and chattily long-winded expression of individual feelings. To which one could reply for a start that a subjectivity which is systematized, that is to say *cultivated* (belonging to culture), subjected to enormous constraints, which themselves had their source in the symbols of the work, has, perhaps, a greater chance of coming close to the literary object than an uncultivated objectivity, blind to itself and sheltering behind literalness as if it were a natural phenomenon. But to tell the truth, that is not exactly what it is all about: criticism is not science: in criticism, it is not the object which must be opposed to the subject, but its predicate. To put it in another way, we shall say that the critic confronts an object which is not the work, but his own language. What relationship can a critic have with language? It is in this area that one must seek to define the 'subjectivity' of the critic.

Classical criticism forms the naive belief that the subject is a 'solid whole', and the relationship between the subject and language is that between a content and an expression. The recourse to symbolic discourse leads, it seems, to an opposite belief: the subject is not an individual plenitude which one is or is not entitled to pour off into language (according to the 'genre' of literature one chooses), but on the contrary a void around which the writer weaves a discourse which is infinitely transformed (that is to say inserted in a chain of transformation), so that all writing *which does not lie* designates not the internal attributes of the subject, but its absence.[89] Language

89 Here one recognizes an echo, though perhaps a distorted one, of the teachings of Dr Lacan in his seminar at the Ecole pratique des Hautes Etudes.

is not the predicate of a subject which is inexpressible or which language serves to signify; language is the subject.[90] It seems to me (and I believe I am not the only one who thinks so) that it is very precisely that which defines literature: if it were simply a matter of expressing (like the juice from a lemon) subjects and objects which are equally solid wholes by 'images', what would be the point of literature? A discourse in bad faith would be sufficient. What carries the symbol along is the necessity of endlessly designating the *nothing* of the *I* that I am. In adding his language to that of the author and his symbols to those of the work, the critic does not 'deform' the object in order to express himself in it, he does not make of it the predicate of his own person; he reproduces yet again, like a sign which is lifted out and varied, the sign of the works themselves, whose message, infinitely repeated, is not a particular 'subjectivity', but the very merging of subject and language, so that criticism and the work always say: *I am literature* and so that through their combined voices, literature never enunciates anything other than the absence of the subject.

To be sure, criticism is a deep reading (or even better: a reading *in cross-section*), it discovers in the work a certain intelligibility, and in that, it is true, it deciphers and participates in an interpretation. However, what it reveals cannot be a signified [signifié] (for this signified retreats endlessly right up to the void of the subject), but only chains of symbols, homologies of relations: the

---

90 '*Only the inexpressible is subjective*', says Picard (p.13). That is to dismiss rather rapidly the relations between subject and language, which 'thinkers' other than Picard consider to be a particularly difficult problem.

'meaning' which it is fully entitled to attribute to the work is finally nothing but a new flowering of the symbols which constitute the work. When a critic draws from the bird and the fan of Mallarmé a common 'meaning', that of *coming and going*, of *virtuality*,[91] he is not designating a final truth about the image but simply a new image, itself suspended. Criticism is not a translation but a periphrase. It cannot claim to rediscover the 'essence' of the work, for this essence is the subject itself, that is to say an absence: every metaphor is a sign without a substance, and it is this far-off quality of the signified that the symbolic process, in its profusion, designates: the critic can only continue the metaphors of the work, not reduce them: once again, if there is in the work a 'buried' and 'objective' signified, the symbol is nothing but euphemism, literature is nothing but disguising and criticism is nothing but philology. It is sterile to bring the work down to pure explicitness, since then *immediately* there is nothing more to say about it and since also the function of the work cannot be to seal the lips of those who read it; but it is hardly less vain to seek in the work what it might be saying without actually saying it and to suppose that it has a final secret, to which, once discovered, there would equally be nothing to add: whatever one says about the work, there always remains in it something of language, of the subject, of absence, *just as there was at the moment of its inception.*

The measure of critical discourse is its *exactness* [justesse]. Just as in music, although a note which is exactly in tune [juste] is not a 'truthful' note, nevertheless the truth of the singing depends, when all's said and done,

91 J.–P. Richard, III, VI.

upon its exactness, because exactness is made up of a certain unison and harmony, so the critic, in order to be true, must be exact[§] and try to reproduce in his own language, according to '*a precise spiritual mise en scène*',[92] the symbolic conditions of the work, failing which, precisely, he cannot 'respect' it. There are indeed two ways, not equally striking, it is true, of missing the symbol. The first, as we have seen, is summary indeed: it consists in denying the existence of the symbol, in reducing the whole signifying profile of the work to the platitudes of a false literalness or in imprisoning it in the impasse of a tautology. At the other extreme, the second consists in interpreting the symbol scientifically: in declaring on the one hand that the work offers itself to be deciphered (in this lies the symbolic character conceded to it), but on the other hand in undertaking this deciphering using a discourse which itself is literal, without depth, closed off, charged with the task of halting the infinite metaphor of the work in order to possess its 'truth' in this standstill: of this type are symbolic modes of criticism with scientific intentions (sociological or psychoanalytic). In both cases it is the absolute disparity between the languages, that of the work and that of the critic, which causes the symbol to be missed: to wish to diminish the symbol is just as excessive as obstinately to refuse to see anything other

---

[§] Translator's note: Barthes's logic here rests partly on the fact that in French 'juste' means correct, exact, true, appropriate etc. as well as meaning 'in tune'. It is thus impossible to render his argument in English.

92 Mallarmé, Preface to 'Un coup de dés jamais n'abolira le hasard', *Oeuvres complètes*, Pléiade, p.455.

than the strict letter. *The symbol must go and seek the symbol*, a language must fully speak another language: it is in this way finally that the letter of the work is respected. This detour which in the end returns the critic to literature is not a vain one: it allows us to fight against a double danger: speaking about a work does indeed expose us to the risk of adopting an empty discourse, either chat, or silence, or else a reifying discourse which immobilizes under a final literal meaning the signified which it believes it has found. In criticism, the right discourse [*la parole juste*] is possible only if the responsibility of the 'interpreter' towards the work becomes the same as the responsibility of the critic towards his own discourse.

Faced with the science of literature, even if he glimpses it, the critic remains infinitely powerless, for he cannot use language as a possession or an instrument: *he is a person who does not know where he stands in relation to the science of literature*. Even if one defined this science to him as being purely a science where things are 'laid bare' (and not an explanatory science), he would still be separated from it: what he lays bare is language itself, not its object. However this distance is not entirely a bad thing, if it allows criticism to develop precisely what is lacking in science; this one could sum up in a word: *irony.* Irony is nothing other than the question which language puts to language.[93] The habit we have adopted of giving a religious or poetic horizon to the symbol prevents us from seeing that there is an irony of symbols, a way of calling

93 In so far as there is a *certain* relationship between the critic and the novelist, the irony of the critic (*vis-à-vis* his own language as a created object) is not fundamentally different

language into question by apparent, declared excesses of language. Confronted with the poverty of Voltairean irony, the narcissistic product of a language with too much confidence in itself, one can imagine another irony which, for want of a better word, we shall call *baroque*, because it makes play with forms and not with beings, because it opens out language instead of shrinking it.[94] Why should irony be forbidden to criticism? It is perhaps the only serious form of discourse which remains available to criticism so long as the status of science and language is not clearly established – which seems to be still the case today. Irony is therefore what is immediately given to the critic: not to see the truth, in Kafka's phrase, but to be it,[95] so that we are entitled to ask him, not *make me believe what you are saying*, but even more, *make me believe in your decision to say it.*

---

from the irony or humour which, according to Lukács,* René Girard and L. Goldmann,* marks the way in which the novelist goes beyond the awareness of his heroes (cf. L. Goldmann, 'Introduction aux problemès d'une sociologie du roman', *Revue de l'Institut de Sociologie*, Bruxelles, 1963, 2, p.229). It goes without saying that this irony (or self-irony) is never perceptible to the opponents of new criticism.

94 Gongorism in the transhistorical sense of the term always has a reflexive element; using tones which can vary greatly, from the oratorical to simple playfulness, the excessive figure of speech contains a reflection on language, whose seriousness is well tested. (Cf. Severo Sarduy, 'Sur Góngora', *Tel Quel*, 25 (printemps 1965), pp.91–93.

95 'Not everyone can see truth, but everyone can be truth...', F. Kafka, quoted by Marthe Robert, p.80.

Part II

Reading

There remains one last illusion which it is necessary to renounce: the critic can in no wise substitute himself for the reader. In vain will he presume – or will others ask him – to lend a voice, however respectful, to the readings of others, to be himself but a reader to whom other readers have delegated the expression of their own feelings as a consequence of his knowledge or his judgment, in other words to exercise by proxy the rights of the community in relation to the work. Why? Because even if one defines the critic as a reader who writes, that means that this reader encounters on his path a redoubtable mediator: writing.

To write, however, is in a certain way to split up the world (the book) and to remake it. Let us think here of the characteristically profound and subtle way in which the Middle Ages had settled the problem of the relationship between the book (treasure from the remote past) and those who had the task of retransmitting this absolute thing (absolutely respected) through another discourse. Today we know only the historian and the critic (and even there we are wrongly asked to believe that we must run the two together); the Middle Ages had established around the book four distinct functions: the *scriptor* (who copied without adding anything), the *compilator* (who never added anything of his own), the *commentator* (who made a personal contribution to the copied text only to render it intelligible) and finally the *auctor* (who gave his own ideas, always justifying his views with reference to other authorities). Such a system, explicitly established with the sole purpose of being 'faithful' to the text from antiquity, the only Book which was recognized (can one imagine greater respect than that of the Middle Ages for Aristotle or Priscianus Caesariensis?),* such a system produced, however, an 'interpretation' of antiquity which modernity has hastened to reject and which would appear to our 'objective' criticism as completely 'delirious'. This is because critical vision begins with the *compilator* himself: it is not necessary to add something of oneself to a text in order to 'distort' it: it suffices to quote it, that is to say, to break it up: a new intelligibility is born immediately; this intelligibility can be accepted by people to a greater or lesser extent: it is none the less a construction. The critic is nothing other than a *commentator*, but he is fully that (and that is enough to put him on dangerous ground): for on the one hand, he is a transmitter, he re-conveys something from the past (this is often necessary: for after all, is not Racine somewhat indebted to Georges Poulet* and Verlaine to Jean-Pierre Richard*?);[96] and on the other hand he is an operator, for he rearranges the elements of the work so as to give it a certain comprehensibility, that is to say a certain distance.

Another separation between the reader and the critic: while we do not know how a reader *speaks* to a book, the critic for his part is obliged to adopt a certain 'tone', and this tone, when all's said and done, can only be affirmative. The critic may well privately doubt and suffer in a thousand ways and about points which are imperceptible to the most malevolent of those who judge him, he can in the last resort have recourse only to writing which is fully writing [une écriture pleine] that is to say assertive writing. It is pointless to claim to avoid the act of starting

---

96 Georges Poulet: 'Notes sur le temps racininien' *Etudes sur le temps humain* Plon, 1950; J.–P. Richard: 'Fadeur de Verlaine', in *Poésie et Profondeur*, Seuil, 1955.

things off which underlies all writing by protestations of modesty, doubt or prudence: those are coded signs, like others: they cannot guarantee anything. Writing *declares*, that is what makes it writing. How, without bad faith, could criticism be interrogative, optative or dubitative, since it is writing and to write is precisely to encounter the categorical[§] risk, the unavoidable alternative of true/false? What the dogmatism of literature – if there is such a thing – declares is a commitment, not a certainty or a complacency: it is nothing but an act, that small amount of act which exists in literature.

Thus 'approaching' a text, not with one's eyes, but with writing, creates an abyss between criticism and reading, which is the very abyss which all meaning creates between its signifying aspect and the aspect which is signified. For nobody knows anything about the sense which reading attributes to the work, nor anything about the signified, perhaps because this sense, being desire, is established beyond the code of language. Only reading loves the work, entertains with it a relationship of desire. To read is to desire the work, to want to be the work, to refuse to echo the work using any discourse other than that of the work: the only commentary which a pure

---

[§] Translator's note: Barthes uses the word 'apophantique' here, which I have translated by 'categorical'. 'Apophantique' is of relatively recent appearance in French (1945) and there appears to be no cognate word in English. It should not be confused with 'apophatic', which means feigning to deny what one really means to assert. 'Apophantique' derives from the Greek adjective 'apophantikos', meaning, in Aristotelian logic, that which can be said to be true or false, or that which is the object of a judgment.

reader could produce, if he were to remain purely a reader, would be a pastiche (as the example of Proust, lover of reading and of pastiches, shows). To go from reading to criticism is to change desires, it is no longer to desire the work but to desire one's own language. But by that very process it is to send the work back to the desire to write from which it arose. And so discourse circulates around the book: *reading*, *writing*: all literature goes from one desire to another. How many writers have written only because they have read? How many critics have read only in order to write? They have brought together the two sides of the book, the two aspects of the sign, so that a single discourse may emerge from them. Criticism is only a moment in the period of history which is beginning and which leads us to unity – to the truth of writing.

February 1966

Background notes

Gaston Bachelard (1884–1962)
Scientist, philosopher and theoretician of literature. Bachelard practised a subjective and poetic kind of literary analysis based on phenomenology. Both the explanation of a work and its ultimate source are to be found in a dreamlike awareness, *rêverie*, which gives privileged access to the understanding of poetic imagery and reveals that images derive from the four elements of ancient philosophy: earth, air, fire and water. For Bachelard the image is neither the expression of an idea nor even a metaphor; it is already language and charged with intrinsic meanings. See for example his *L'Eau et les rêves* (1942), *L'Air et les songes* (1943), *La Poétique de la rêverie* (1960).

Georges Bataille (1897–1962)
Writer influenced by Hegel, Marx, Nietzsche and Sade who was drawn initially to both mysticism and surrealism. He founded several journals, notably *Acéphale* (1937) and *Critique* (1946) and was interested in sociology. He rejected traditional forms of literature and was led in his writings on creative art – *Lascaux, ou la naissance de l'art* (1955), *La Littérature et le Mal* (1957) – to claim that art should transgress all taboos, especially the two major taboos, those surrounding eroticism and

death. Bataille wrote both essays, for example, *L'Expérience intérieure* (1943), *La Part maudite* (1949), *L'Erotisme* (1957) and fiction, such as *Histoire de l'oeil* (1928), *Madama Edwarda* (1941), *L'Abbé C...* (1950). Bataille believed that art constituted a kind of religious transgression of interdict, and his novels lay emphasis on the spiritual dimension of eroticism rather than on obscenity as such. His conception of eroticism connects in turn with his idea of literature in *La Littérature et le Mal*, where writing is portrayed as an act of communication between the isolated beings who are the author and reader.

Julien Benda (1867–1956)
French writer and philosopher. Friend of Charles Péguy and contributor to Péguy's *Cahiers de la Quinzaine*, which opposed secularism and positivism and argued for a religiously based socialism. Some of Benda's essays, like *La Trahison des clercs* (1927) and *La France byzantine ou le triomphe de la littérature pure* (1945), sought to defend absolute values and the purity of reason against change and evolution. From his earliest writings he adopted, in the name of reason, a stance of refusing whatever smacked of emotion, intuition or sensation. He violently opposed the intuitionist philosophy of Henri Bergson and saw in contemporary writers (Proust, Gide, Valéry) evidence of literary decadence. Benda is no doubt mentioned by Barthes as an example of a kind of nostalgia for rationalism which to Barthes was even more inappropriate in 1965 than in Benda's day.

Maurice Blanchot (b.1907)
Whether in his novels – *Thomas l'obscur* (1941),

Aminadab (1942), *Le Très-Haut* (1948), in *Le dernier Homme* (1957) his *recits* (short fictional narratives written in the first person by a narrator who is also an author), or in his critical essays, *La Part du feu* (1949), *L'Espace littéraire* (1955), *Le Livre à venir* (1959) – Blanchot highlights the ambiguous and problematical nature of language. He is interested in the creative process and in the relationship between a work and the silence which precedes or surrounds it. For Blanchot, writing celebrates not objects but their absence. Influenced by the Romantics and Nietzsche, Blanchot links literature to the exploration of the impossible, of nothingness, of death, of existence. Blanchot's vertiginous reflections on language and the primacy he accords to the written text have influenced many modern writers, both novelists (the *nouveau roman*) and critics like the new critics and Barthes himself.

Georges Blin (b.1917)
Professor of modern French literature at the Collège de France from 1965. Like Richard and Poulet, he is one of the 'new critics' who look for recurring themes in works of art. He has written important works on poetry – *Baudelaire* (1939), *Le Sadisme de Baudelaire* (1948) and the novel – *Stendhal et les problèmes du roman* (1958), *Stendhal et les problèmes de la personnalité* (1958) which show an interest in the psychology of the writer as well as in the construction and inspirational sources of works of art.

Nicolas Boileau (1636–1711)
French classical writer. Theoretician of poetry in his *Art poétique* (1674). In the aesthetic debate of his time, the

Querelle des Anciens et des Modernes, (dispute concerning the relative merits of classical and modern writers), he sided with those who defended the superiority of the writers of classical antiquity over modern authors. If he supported the '*Anciens*' in that famous debate, it was because he saw little value in contemporary writers apart from Molière and Racine, whose friend and loyal supporter he was. (The complexity of the *Querelle* is shown by the fact that Molière and Racine themselves were staunch supporters of the virtues of the 'Anciens', whose models they tried to emulate.) Fontenelle (1657–1757) was the best known defender of the *Modernes*, especially in his *Digression sur les Anciens et les Modernes* (1688) in which he argued that poetry could not imitate the classical pagan models and should rather adopt new forms more in accordance with the spirit of the age.

Ferdinand Brunetière (1849–1906)
Professor, critic and historian of literature. He sought to apply to literature the same scientific rigour which he saw in Darwin's presentation of his concept of evolution. Brunetière is credited with having created the history of genres, which he applied to criticism itself in *Evolution de la critique* (1890). Loyal to what he perceived as the sure values of the French classical period, he was hostile to most of the literary movements of his century, including naturalism, symbolism, the excesses of romanticism and the doctrine of 'art for art's sake'.

Avram Noam Chomsky (b.1928)
Professor of modern languages and general linguistics at Massachusetts Institute of Technology since 1955. His

first published book, *Syntactic Structures* (1957), argues that structural linguistics is based upon an inadequate theory of knowledge. The changes he has brought to the discipline of linguistics have been considered so radical by some as to be described as a Copernican revolution. Chomsky's transformational grammar introduces his ideas of *creativity* and *grammaticality*: all native speakers of a language have an intuition of its structure which allows them to distinguish grammatical from ungrammatical usage and to understand and articulate an infinite number of new sentences.

Other important works by Chomsky are *Current Issues in Linguistic Theory* (1964) in which he contrasts transformational grammar with the 'taxonomic' model of the structuralists. In *Aspects of the Theory of Syntax* (1965) he further develops his views on syntax, phonology and semantics in the wider framework of generative grammar. *Cartesian Linguistics* (1966) acknowledges his debt to Humboldt and to the grammarians of Port-Royal. In *Language and Mind* (1968) he relates his theories of syntax to a general theory of the psychology of knowledge. His later works, such as *The Sound Pattern of English* (co-author M. Halle, 1968), *Studies on Semantics in Generative Grammar* (1972) and *Reflections on Language* (1976), develop and refine aspects of his theories and defend them against attacks.

Chomsky's views of language seem to represent for Barthes a scientific model which can be applied *mutatis mutandis* to literature. Literary works can be viewed as instances of a rule, as exemplars derived from an infinite logically possible series of unrealized literary works. For Barthes, the work could be evidence of a 'literature faculty' in people just as for Chomsky the correctly formulated sentence is evidence of a 'language faculty'.

Barthes finds a fruitful application in literary theory for the notions of creativity, and of intuition of conformity with a rule, which Chomsky originally developed in the context of language.

Chrysale
A character from Molière's *Les Femmes savantes* (1672), who represents a reactionary and down-to-earth commonsense attitude.

Demetrius Phalereus (c.BC 350–283)
Athenian orator and statesman. His works have all perished but he was considered a fine stylist.

Lucien Febvre (1878–1956)
French historian, professor at the Collège de France from 1933 and at the Ecole pratique des Hautes Etudes from 1947. His first published work, a thesis entitled *Philippe II et la Franche-Comté* (1911) already revealed his desire to show the links between different disciplines. History is conceived not as a series of facts but as an account of the inter-connection between geography, the social sciences, religion and culture as they influence human behaviour. Febvre was interested in religious thought in the sixteenth century and published a number of studies, for example, *Un Destin, Martin Luther* (1928), *Le Problème de l'incroyance au XVIe siècle* (1942), *La Religion de Rabelais* (1942).

Febvre is principally remembered for his emphasis on history as a broad-ranging and synthetic discipline. In this connection he was associated with the journal *Revue de synthèse*; he also launched an encyclopedia, the *Encyc-*

lopédie française (1933). Most of all, he is identified with the important journal *Annales* which he founded in 1929 with Marc Bloch; its later change of title to *Annales, économies, sociétés, civilisations* is itself evidence of Febvre's conception of history.

Michel Foucault (1926–84)
French philosopher and historian of ideas. He taught at several universities and was then appointed to the Collège de France in 1970. His celebrated *Histoire de la folie à l'âge classique, folie et déraison* (1961) articulated the view that the dichotomy which developed in the seventeenth century between order and reason on the one hand and disorder and unreason on the other, showed that each society feels constrained to mark off that which is separate from itself. He pursued the analysis in *La Naissance d'une clinique, une archéologie du regard médical* (1963). The notion of archaeology is critical in Foucault's thought. Adopting a 'structuralist' approach, he presents a model of human understanding as being constituted in layers corresponding to different periods, each layer requiring its own epistemological approach. See *Les Mots et les choses, une archéologie du savoir humain* (1966) and *Archéologie du savoir* (1969). Some important later works are *Surveiller et punir, naissance de la prison* (1975) and the three-volume *Histoire de la sexualité* (1976, 1984, 1984).

Alain Girard (b.1914)
French demographer and sociologist. Girard is a professor at the Sorbonne and technical adviser at the Institut national d'Etudes Démographiques. In addition to the book *Le Journal intime* (1963) mentioned by Barthes in

his text, Girard has written various works on behaviour and social attitudes – *La Réussite sociale en France* (1961), *Le Choix du conjoint en France* (1964) and on the electoral process.

Barthes mentions Girard as an example of one type of approach among others – in this case, the sociological approach – which can be brought to bear upon a text or a genre.

Saint-Marc Girardin (1801–73)
Professor at the Sorbonne and critic. He was an opponent of romanticism and a defender of classical values from a specifically moral viewpoint.

Lucien Goldmann (1913–70)
French Marxist critic and philosopher, born in Romania. Director of studies at the Ecole pratique des Hautes Etudes. Influenced by Freud, Lukács and Jean Piaget, Goldmann developed a new approach to the sociological study of literature. He called his method 'genetic structuralism', to distance it from mainstream or what he called 'static' structuralism which in his view failed to understand the dynamic relationship between mental and social structures. Goldmann's thesis is that there is a non-conscious reproduction by a great writer in his work of mental structures homologous to those which exist in society. (This relationship is one of a parallel between similar entities; unlike most Marxist critics, Goldmann rejects the idea that a work 'reflects' society or social structures.) Like Lukács, Goldmann believed that criticism was an exercise in 'totalization'; the critic must account for the work in its entirety, including its aesthetic unity. The critic must also be aware of both the author's

consciousness – which in a capitalist economy will necessarily be alienated and divided against itself – and of the broader society, which, in Goldmann's view, is the ultimate creator of works of art.

His major works are: *La Communauté humaine et l'univers chez Kant* (1948), *Le Dieu caché: étude sur la vision tragique dans 'Les Pensées' de Pascal and dans le théâtre de Racine* (1955), *Pour une sociologie du roman* (1964) and *Structures mentales et création culturelle* (1970).

Guermantes
The name of an aristocratic family, and of the village where they have their château, in Proust's novel *A la recherche du temps perdu* (1913–27).

Wilhelm von Humboldt (1767–1835)
German linguist. Under the influence of Chomsky the twentieth century has seen a revival of interest in his theories of language. For Humboldt, language is not a simple reflection of pre-existing reality, but the faculty which allows us to organize the world. The faculty of language is an innate property inherent in the human mind: it is the 'organ which forms thought'. Humboldt's idea that there is a language faculty interests Barthes for the same reason that Chomsky's views concern him: Barthes is tempted to draw an analogy between an innate capacity to structure the world linguistically and an innate capacity to make and comprehend literature.

Roman Jakobson (1896–1982)
Russian-born linguist and critic, originally connected with Russian Formalism through the Moscow Linguistic

Circle, who applied linguistics to the study of literary language. After working with the Prague Linguistic Circle in the 1920s and 1930s he lived for a time in Denmark and Norway, working with the Linguistic Circle in Copenhagen. During World War II he emigrated to the USA, where he taught in New York, at Harvard and at the Massachusetts Institute of Technology. In his American period he was no longer associated with a definite school, but was still generally considered to be part of the structuralist movement, publishing widely on a range of linguistic and literary problems. An interdisciplinary scholar *par excellence*, he undertook research in many areas of literature and linguistics: phonology, language acquisition in children (and its destruction by aphasia), the relationship between communication theory and the structure of language (theory of the functions of language), poetic language and literary theory. The most important articles from his considerable output have been regrouped in four volumes of *Selected Writings* (I *Phonological Studies*; II *Word and Language*; III *The Poetry of Grammar and the Grammar of Poetry*; IV *Slavic Epic Studies*).

Access to Jakobson for the French reader was greatly facilitated by the publication of the first volume of his *Selected Writings* in a French translation in 1963 – *Essais de linguistique générale*, I (1963). Volume II followed in 1973. Barthes's *Critique et vérité*, appearing as it did in 1966, was both a product of, and a contributor to, the growing French interest in problems in structuralism and linguistics and their relationship to literature, issues which were being explored by thinkers such as Jakobson.

La Berma
Fictional actress written about by Proust in *A la recherche du temps perdu*. The name apparently combines references to Sarah Bernhardt and to the tragic actress Réjane whom Proust had admired in his youth.

Jacques Lacan (1901–81)
French psychiatrist , psychoanalyst and theorist. A disciple of Freud, he was a teacher of psychiatry at the Sainte-Anne Hospital for ten years and then appointed to the Ecole pratique des Hautes Etudes (1963). He withdrew from all international psychiatric societies and founded the Ecole Freudienne de Paris in 1964 and then dissolved it in 1980 after internal power struggles, arguing that his colleagues were too conformist. Lacan adopted original positions in psychoanalytic theory from as early as 1936, when he developed ideas on the importance of the 'mirror stage', in psycho-sexual development. His teaching was essentially oral but has been partly collected in the books *Ecrits* (1966) and *Séminaire* (1975). Two important notions which underlie his work are the ideas, first, that the unconscious reflects the way other people reason and speak, and secondly, that the unconscious is structured like a language. (This latter idea is of course of particular interest to Barthes who was seeking analogues for the way literature is structured.) Lacan's emphasis on desire, as part of the problem of the relationship to the other, seems also to have influenced Barthes. At the end of *Criticism and Truth* Barthes alludes to the vague no man's land where reading, desire and the work meet.

Lautréamont, Count of (Isidore Ducasse) (1846–70)
Poet and dreamer, a precursor of surrealism often likened

to Rimbaud. He wrote little, leaving for posterity a handful of letters, a few poems, and the *Chants de Maldoror* (1869) in which coexist a refusal of conventional values and great poetic sensibility.

Népomucène Lemercier (1771–1840)
Prolific author, especially of theatre. His theory of drama emphasized his belief in realistic portrayal of character and in the need to blend comedy and tragedy.

Claude Lévi-Strauss (b.1908)
Anthropologist. Director of Studies at the Ecole pratique des Hautes Etudes from 1950, Professor at the Collège de France (1959–82). *Tristes tropiques* (1955) gives an account of his early professional life as an ethnologist in Brazil and Pakistan in the 1930s and 1940s. In *Sociologie et anthropologie* (1950) he first gives an indication that Saussurean structural linguistics could fruitfully be applied to anthropology. (Saussure's original conception of structural linguistics was built upon by Jakobson, whom Lévi-Strauss met during seven years' exile in New York from 1941.) Other important works are the articles 'L'Analyse structurale en linguistique et en anthropologie' (1945), which enunciates the theoretical bases of his future structural anthropology and *Social structure* (1952, in English; 1958 in French as *Les limites de la notion de structure en éthnologie*). Lévi-Strauss analysed social structures and practises in works like *Les Structures élémentaires de la parenté* (1949) *Anthropologie structurale* (1958) and *Anthropologie structurale II* (1973). The structural method was also used to study systems of classification in *Le Totémisme aujourd'hui* (1962), and *La Pensée sauvage* (1962).

The article 'La Structure des mythes' (1955), marks a turning-point in the elaboration of structural philosophy and its application to myth. A comparative approach to myth is inadequate and unrevealing, declares Lévi-Strauss. If myths have a meaning, then that meaning emerges not from an examination of their separate elements but from the way in which those elements are *combined*. Formal properties, such as binary relationships, are given prominence, and their repetition and re-combination highlighted. A series of works, *Le Cru et le cuit* (1964), *Du Miel aux cendres* (1967), *L'Origine des manières de table* (1968) and *L'Homme nu* (1971), constitute an examination of more than 800 myths, principally American-Indian, the passage from one to another being negotiated by what Lévi-Strauss calls 'transformations'. In the final phase of his work Lévi-Strauss applies structural analysis to figurative representation in American-Indian culture – *La Voie des masques* (1975).

György Lukács (1885–1971)
Hungarian philosopher and critic. His main works are *The Soul and the Forms* (1911) (written in Hungarian), a pre-Marxist work; *Die Theorie des Romans* (1920, written in German) an examination influenced by Hegel of the relationship between history and aesthetic forms; *Geschichte und Klassenbewusstsein* (1923, written in German); *Studies in European Realism* (1948, written in Hungarian), a view of the world as an objective datum reflected in the consciousness of the artist; *The Historical Novel* (1947, written in Hungarian) and *Goethe and his time* (1946, written in Hungarian), which are based on admiration of Balzac and Tolstoy as 'great realist writers', and of Goethe as a product of the German Enlightenment

and rationalism. Influenced first by Hegel and then by Marx, Lukács highlighted two concepts, that of *totality* and that of *alienation*. The category of totality, the belief that the whole is more important than all the parts, implies that an overall analysis of cultural or economic phenomena is necessary. This analysis must lay due importance on human consciousness and, according to Lukács, the privileged form of consciousness during the capitalist phase is that of the exploited proletariat. From the young Marx Lukács borrowed the concept of alienation, and developed the idea that under capitalism people have become pure objects, valued only for their place in a market economy. Only socialist revolution will free them.

Lukács has been one of the most important Marxist critics and writers of the twentieth century, influential not so much in Hungary as in Western European critical circles. Lucien Goldmann, for example, openly acknowledged his debt to him. A man of international interests and wide general culture (he lived for a time in Germany and the Soviet Union as well as in his native Hungary), Lukács was by no means an orthodox Marxist critic. His works have fallen in and out of favour behind the Iron Curtain.

Stéphane Mallarmé (1842–98)
French poet and one of the main figures in the Symbolist movement. Mallarmé saw himself as forging a new poetic language: in a letter to a friend in October 1894 he wrote of his terror as he approached the task of writing a major new poem, 'Hérodiade' - 'I'm inventing a language which must burst forth from a new poetics, which I can briefly sum up as: depicting not the object itself but the effect it produces (*peindre non la chose mais l'effet qu'elle produit*)'. Literary composition for him was a task rooted

in anguish. Transfixed by the blank page and by the difficulty of fixing the absolute in words, he never wrote the Great Book (*le Grand Livre*) which was to sum up his thoughts. He left a small number of often sensual but usually extremely enigmatic poems, famous among which is 'L'Après-midi d'un faune'.

Maurice Merleau-Ponty (1908–61)
French philosopher. Held a chair in psychology and pedagogy at the Sorbonne (1949–52) and was a professor at the Collège de France from 1952. In philosophical psychology he was a phenomenologist and influenced by Hegel and Husserl; as a moral and political thinker he was linked with existentialism. With Sartre he founded the journal *Les Temps Modernes* after World War II and was sympathetic to Marxism, but the discovery of the existence of prison camps in the USSR led to a split with Sartre which was both political and philosophical. He developed a 'philosophy of understanding' which was pluralist rather than dogmatic. Important works: *La Structure du comportement* (1942), *Phénoménologie de la perception* (1945), *Humanisme et terreur* (1947), *Sens et non-sens* (1948), *Les Aventures de la dialectique* (1955), *L'Oeil et l'esprit* (1964), *Le Visible et l'invisible* (1964).

Désiré Nisard (1806–88)
Critic and professor at the Sorbonne and at the Collège de France. Author of a *Histoire de la littérature française* (1844–61) which valued only the writers of the French classical period (the seventeenth century). He believed in the genius of France and the French language and proclaimed that criticism was an exact science. His ideas

were reflected in the way literature was taught in French schools and universities in the nineteenth and early twentieth centuries.

Georges Poulet (b.1902)
Belgian-born critic who is a leading member of the so-called Geneva school of criticism. He is the exponent of a thematic criticism which rests on the one hand on a partial identification with the consciousness of the author, and on the other, on the perception of a number of organizing categories in the work (e.g. time, space, the circle). For Poulet, the critic's task is to 'replace the confused movement of existence by a precise intellectual schema which is its intellectual equivalent'. His principal works are *Etudes sur le temps humain* (1950–71), *Les Métamorphoses du cercle* (1961), *Mesure de l'instant* (1968), *Entre moi et moi* (1977), *La Poésie éclatée* (1980).

Priscianus Caesariensis
Latin grammarian of the fifth or sixth century AD. His grammar was the basis of Latin teaching in the Middle Ages.

Raymond Queneau (1903–76)
French writer. For a time part of the surrealist movement. A philologist and mathematician as well as a novelist and poet, he had a whimsical sense of humour, a playful attitude to language and a liking for producing endless permutations and combinations as he experimented with style. He was a novelist (see particularly *Zazie dans le métro*, (1959)) and a poet, but his most famous, and essentially unclassifiable works are *Exercices de style* (1947) and *Cent Mille Milliards de poèmes* (1961).

Jean-Pierre Richard (b.1922)
French literary critic. Now Professor of literature at Vincennes, part of the University of Paris. He is the author of many studies, principally of nineteenth- and twentieth-century novelists and poets. Richard is a thematic critic who considers an author's semi-private world of sensation and sensibility to be both the source and the essential subject of his works. He is interested in recapturing the creative moment, 'when the world takes on a meaning through the act which describes it'. His principal works are: *Littérature et sensation* (1954), *Poésie et profondeur* (1955), *L'Univers imaginaire de Mallarmé* (1961), *Onze études sur la poésie moderne* (1967), *Le Paysage de Chateaubriand* (1967), *Proust et le monde sensible* (1974).

Second Empire
Rule of Louis Napoleon (Napoleon III), who was Emperor of France from 1852 to 1870, and discouraged experiments in both political and literary freedom.

Philippe Sollers (b.1936)
French literary theorist and writer. Editor of the journal *Tel Quel*, founded in 1960. *Tel Quel*'s ideological positions have ranged from the interest in aesthetics and poetry shown in the first edition, through a concern with Nietzsche and Marx, to the problems of structuralism and the status of the text. The journal has refused to identify with any school of thought whether structuralist or Marxist – and has indeed condemned nearly all Marxist régimes as being opposed to Marx's own principles. As a novelist, Sollers moved from a conventional beginning with *Le Défi* (1957) and *Une Curieuse Solitude* (1958) to

an open experimentation with language and viewpoint in novels such as *Nombres* (1968), *Lois* (1972) and *H* (1973). Sollers feels he is subverting the Western bourgeois ideology by writing novels which question writing practice and conservative beliefs and his novels are intended to be 'open' texts. His latest novel is *Portrait du joueur* (1984). Soller's essays are complementary to his novels. *Logiques* (1968) is a collection of essays which Sollers has said should be read 'simultaneously and dialectically' with his novel *Nombres*. Sollers's more openly political essays written since 1968 like *Sur le matérialisme* (1974) show a continuing concern to treat literature as part of politics and society and not as mere *belles-lettres*.

Hippolyte Taine (1828–93)
Historian, philosopher and critic who was the author of numerous lengthy works. As a critic he sought to explain the few 'eternal passions' which guide humankind, by relating particular writers to the general categories of 'race, milieu et moment' ('race' – a concept of cultural identity based on nationality, physical characteristics, language, religion, etc. – social environment and point of time). The work of art arises from the way in which the organizing faculty of the writer responds to these three influences (see the preface to his *Histoire de la littérature anglaise* (1863). For him criticism was a kind of science, a 'sort of botany applied not to plants but to human works'. Taine is now associated with the search for origins, and the wish to generalize and synthesize.

Index